CAFETERIA

NEW IDENTITIES IN

AMERICA
CONTEMPORARY LIFE

June Sochen

Iowa State University Press / Ames

To Joyce and Leonard Schrager

June Sochen is Professor of History at Northeastern Illinois University.

© 1988 Iowa State University Press, Ames, Iowa 50010
All rights reserved

Composed by Iowa State University Press
Printed in the United States of America

First edition, 1988

Library of Congress Cataloging-in-Publication Data
Sochen, June, 1937–
    Cafeteria America: new identities in contemporary life / June Sochen. — 1st ed.
    p.   cm.
    Bibliography: p.
    ISBN 0-8138-0255-5
    1. United States—Popular culture—History—20th century. 2. United States—Civilization—1970–   . 3. Women—United States—Social conditions. 4. Children—United States—Social conditions. I. Title.
E169.12.S63   1988   87-35378
973.92—dc19   CIP

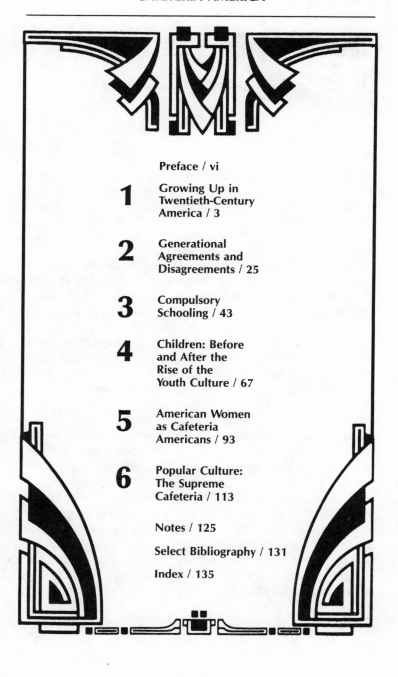

PREFACE

Cafeteria America is a collection of essays on subjects that have preoccupied my mind for many years. American women have been the subject of my research, writing, lecturing, and teaching for the past eighteen years. My interest in popular culture probably dates back to my adolescent movie-going days; my concern for defining and understanding the American character is inextricably tied to my interest in the story of American women. The themes of American values—past, present, and future—the role of both sexes in American life, and the traits of the American family all inevitably interact with the study of women.

In the course of my intellectual pursuits, I have been struck by the similarities and differences in growing up in America. Because of traditional views on the sexes, girls and boys have been raised with different expectations, dreams, and opportunities. Girls and boys imbibed popular cultural images, attended classes, and learned parental messages that spoke of essential differences in their respective adult destinies. *Cafeteria America* explores some of these preoccupying themes within self-contained but related essays.

As a cultural historian, I am interested in discussing the major factors, as I see them, that reshaped and reinterpreted the traditional identity-forming institutions. It is usually the sociologists and psychologists who boldly describe the prototypical American. The historian avoids the big generalization for the precise analysis of a particular person, time, and place. It is the psychologist who analyzes what is normal and abnormal about the American personality, while the sociologist describes group patterns of behavior.

It is a rare cultural historian indeed, such as David Potter, who ventured an analysis of the American character, the identity problem writ large. His study, *People of Plenty,* is an extremely insightful foray into the role abundance has played in forming the American character. He has had few imitators or followers. Yet personality and national character studies (unfashionable in current historical circles) are a legitimate enterprise for cultural historians interested in understanding the unique features of Americans. By defining and analyzing the factors that shape the development of American personalities, the historian can contribute to an understanding of who contemporary Americans are and how they came into being.

Choices, or the semblance of choices, are the essence of a cafeteria. In our culture, where the democratic rhetoric speaks of equal opportunity, there is also the implicit assumption that there are opportunities ready to be seized upon by the inventive individual. Popular culture offers seemingly endless choices. In the popular cafeteria, even women are offered choices: they can remake themselves and they can retrieve their losses. Women's roles can be diverse and ever changing, though the sameness within the change offers assurances to audiences that all will be well in the end.

Potter's *People of Plenty* described the sheer riches of

the American environment and culture. What I am suggesting is that the cafeteria of popular culture expresses itself in particular and peculiar ways when considering women's images: it suggests variety and choice while sometimes confirming traditional views of women. *Cafeteria America* explores the interconnections between various cultural trends and institutions; the result of the interaction, I suggest, is the creation of a new national personality type—the cafeteria personality. Within this context, various subcultural institutions may act as countervailing forces: religious and reform groups may provide anchors, guides, and goals for lives that would otherwise be taken over by the temptations of the cafeteria. The dominant recreational culture contributes to the cafeteria quality of the American personality.

First children, and then later in this century, women, have been lured into the riches of the cafeteria; eventually, then, everyone is affected. The nationalizing trends, combined with the subcultural entertainment/leisure-time force, subjects to be discussed in the following pages, have produced the new American personality; the latter is an audacious generalization that will be my task to document. *Cafeteria America* operates on a high level of generalization, one I hope readers will be comfortable with and will find congenial to further exploration and discussion.

As in every enterprise, I am grateful to many people who have encouraged and aided me in my work—to my students at Northeastern Illinois University, whose papers and comments in my courses have been invaluable, to Alan M. Schroder for his helpful editorial suggestions, and to my family who are always lively inspirations to me. I thank them all. Ultimately, of course, the views in *Cafeteria America* are mine, for which I assume full responsibility.

CAFETERIA AMERICA

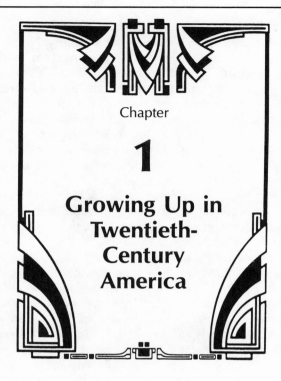

Chapter

1

Growing Up in Twentieth-Century America

Americans, like all other peoples, are culture bound. This is not a condemnation. It is an acknowledgement of the power of cultural values and structures to shape our lives. It is a declaration of an often unpopular notion that each culture is different, unique in some ways, and always terribly influential upon its members. This forthright claim does not deny the power and importance of transcultural, or universal, human traits. Obviously, the only way nations communicate with each other is on the basis of shared human–universal themes. The bounds of culture are not insurmountable; they do not obliterate the ability to share larger concerns.

The culture-bound concept, understandable and free of controversy on one level, often evokes strong disagreement from historians who emphasize transcultural factors to explain American (and indeed everyone's) history. Marxist historians as well as Freudians see the Western world as sharing essential cultural characteristics. They would strongly refute the view that American cultural history is a worthy way to study American history. Rather, they argue that economic self-interest or imperialistic policy determines a country's history. The relationship between the powerful and the powerless is the unrelenting story of each nation's past. In my perspective, the complex mosaic of American culture includes our economic system, our political system, our social system, and all other systems; but all of these discrete units fit into a larger whole, share essential traits with each other, and become compatible threads in the gestalt we call American culture.

By taking a cultural view of history, all expressions are seen as emerging from the complex culture; idiosyncratic and unique themes are culturally motivated as are the representative and mainstream. The ideas and values that are truly different appear as unAmerican in the cultural sense of the term, that is, as inspired by foreign, subversive, minority, and unpopular cultural sources. The truly unusual angle of vision becomes impossible within this scheme; rather, most behavior appears to be culturally determined, arising dialectically from imaginations that probe cultural alternatives. This results, at times, in a strange and fascinating mix of old and new, native and foreign influences.

Indeed, in the continuous interaction of events, of past and present, and of the generations, classes, sexes, and races, old values are transformed and presented in new packages. In the United States, where newness is the highest virtue (a cultural generalization), the old must always be offered in seemingly original and novel form to be accepted. Diplomats invent new slogans as do advertisers, but the underlying messages are often traditional, conventional, and worn. But in this sense, the possibilities for continuity *and* change arise out of the culture, though often in unexpected and unpredictable combinations.

Americans are influenced by both overarching cultural institutions and values and by subcultural forms that remain vibrant and engaging. They watch television, a national cultural institution; they go to school, another national cultural institution; and they attend the church of their choice, a subcultural form. When they watch or play baseball, they are participating in more subcultural forms of behavior; when they jog, lift weights, or race cars, they belong to subcultural groups that give them part of their identity while occupying part of their time. Subcultures, by definition, affect some Americans some of the time, while national cultural institutions and values pervade the whole culture continuously.

The enduring view that each sex has specific adult roles is both culturally determined and a feature of most cultures over time and space. In the American culture, the democratic rhetoric has coexisted with the ideological view that women's primary social roles are that of wife and mother. And the reality, until recently, upheld the dominant cultural view. In this culture, in stark contrast to most others, the clash between democratic individualism and sexist ideology created an active feminist movement while advanced technology opened up life opportunities for women unknown elsewhere.

While all cultures base their practices upon biological, economic, and geographic realities, it is in American culture that the combination of ideology and circumstance has led to more changes for women and minorities than anywhere else.

Thanks to compulsory schooling, one of the subjects of this book, education has become a national cultural trait shared by children all over America. Immigrant children from the Lower East Side in New York as well as middle-class children in Chicago went to school for longer and longer periods, thus sharing a set of values and way of life. They became targets for the growing marketers of this country. They also, over time, assumed more and more powers over their own lives, to the consternation and dismay of their parents.

As will be suggested, another feature of American culture has emerged in the late twentieth century: the cafeteria personality. The structures, the rhetoric, and the ideology of American life have come to accept eclecticism as the pervading pose of Americans. As eclectic cafeteria goers, Americans pick and choose many activities, identities, and roles. They do this while often proclaiming allegiance to tried-and-true values. Women seek new identities in this new environment of endless change and opportunity. In the complex process of evolving as individuals and as group members, Americans bring their cultural lessons to new experiences, reinterpreting the old within new contexts, and amalgamating their views and themselves into renewing creatures. Indeed, mobility, in a social, individual, and geographic sense characterize Americans like no other people. The movement and change that results, however, is not even-paced nor applicable to all parts of the personality or the community; hence the fragmented, or what I call, the cafeteria nature of the late twentieth-century American personality.

While the cafeteria metaphor hangs over the whole culture, there are a variety of relationships between cultural and subcultural institutions and values; they can share and enforce each other's views; they can benignly ignore each other; or they can clash. Most Americans, an ambitious claim, pay lip service to public education, the rule of law, and individual freedom. Some subcultural institutions, such as the Roman Catholic Church in America, prefer parochial education for their children and politely operate in parallel with the dominant culture on this issue.

There are three large areas of subcultural forms, what I call the three Rs: religion, recreation, and reform. Though not all-encompassing, they include a good deal of American subcultural activity. Most Americans identify with a religious group; nearly all enjoy, actively or passively, some form of recreation; and fewer still join reform movements. They do these things while also being influenced by the American Dream myth. In *Cafeteria America,* the recreation subculture is a major focus. Neither reform nor religion applies to my major concern; namely, looking at the development of the cafeteria personality. Besides the recreation subculture, certain nationalizing trends already alluded to (such as compulsory schooling for children, the ideology toward women, and surplus capitalism) will be discussed.

It is within the recreation subculture that the myriad of entertainments, fads, and fashions emerges. It is from here that Americans choose the variety of activities and enjoyments they pursue, often with great fervor. Because this branch of American culture has grown so dramatically in this century, it plays a major role in the creation of the cafeteria personality. Ethnic entertainers, a worthy example of recreational performers, can use the language, the idiom, the intonation, and the style of their particular ethnic group as long as they play only to their own audiences. As soon as they appear on Broadway, on television, or in the movies, they must give up their dialect, ethnic mannerisms, and ethnic material. Americans enjoy performers who represent them in the larger community as well as admire their ability to transcend their particular subculture and "make it" in national culture. When Bertha Kalich, a great Yiddish actress, left her Yiddish audiences for the English stage, she also left behind her exaggerated gestures and her Yiddishisms. As one critic approvingly noted, "Within the past year Madame Kalich has eradicated from her English speech practically the last trace of foreign accent. Her diction is truly beautiful."[1] Indeed, it was only when Madame Kalich gave up her ethnic language that she became acceptable to Broadway.

As popular entertainments grew in number and variety, Americans discovered that they could retain their love for polkas while enjoying vaudeville. They could sample exotic, subcultural recreations as well as blander national fare. They could participate in various cafeterias of entertainment. The pace of change, the very expectation of constant change, would become a major feature of popular culture as well as other areas of American culture. The cafeteria metaphor would rise in each and every dimension of American life. What began in the recreational arena moved into all other arenas of life.

Only elite subcultures, who pride themselves upon their exclusiveness and their separateness, avoid expansion or contact with other groups. Otherwise, the urge of a subculture to become a national cultural form exists in some force. However, in their essence, subcultural institutions or organizations enjoy their particularity. Opera buffs do not expect all operas to be sung in English and television soap opera fans can share the news of their favorite stars and programs without apology or defensiveness to outsiders. Americans, in their cafeteria approach to life, engage in many different subcultural activities during the course of a week or a month and ably keep all of the parts distinct. Indeed, the organization of American culture into competing and cooperative subcultures, alongside a powerful national culture, is the very essence of a cafeteria writ large.

By taking a cultural and subcultural approach to an understanding of American history, many themes and activities can be reinterpreted. Women's history, for example, is seen as part of a larger cultural view of the family, of sex roles, and of individual development. Most women identify with both dominant cultural and subcultural institutions. They belong to families and churches; they participate in the work place; and they enjoy conventional entertainments. Feminist reformers, critics of the cultural status quo, on the other hand, are outsiders; they are a minority of American women who reject the dominant cultural arrangements between the sexes and seek new roles, values, and responsibilities for both sexes. They are a distinct subculture striving to influence the majority to adopt their values and practices.

Feminists, as a subcultural expression, reflect the keenest struggles of living within traditional roles while trying to define new ones. Thus, they become dramatic indicators of the tensions existing between dominant cultural traits and minority reformist values. Like other reformer-outsider groups in American history, the feminists can be assessed for their successes and failures. The passage of desired laws, the realignment of human opportunities, and the reorganization of the family structure can be studied to determine the effectiveness of feminism on the cultural mainstream. Material and technological changes in the environment, of course, often intrude upon this complicated process. The introduction of birth-control pills, the growth of the clerical sector of the economy, and the rise in education for both sexes has had unforeseen consequences for all Americans.

As long as feminists remained a subcultural group, they appeared as outsiders on the fringe of society. Susan B. Anthony and Elizabeth Cady Stanton, struggling to convince women and men as to women's right to vote, were minority women, members of a valiant but modest subcultural group who desperately sought members for their cause. As women's rights and women's lives became more and more like men's rights and lives (more education, jobs outside the home, similar sports and leisure activities), the feminists found much of their campaign absorbed into the cultural mainstream. The feminists, who remained a minority subcultural group, stressed the most unpopular, controversial causes, not yet accepted by the majority of men and women. They were, and are, like other unpopular critics of the cultural majority, important voices of opposition.

Sometimes, the values and goals of a dissident subculture, such as the feminists, will be absorbed in partial and inconsistent ways by majority members, thus resulting in the cafeteria personality. In a 1981 study done by the Social Science Research Council at the University of Michigan called "Juggling Contradictions: Women's Ideas About Families," the researchers noted: "Instead of finding categories of women, we found categories of ideas . . . bits and pieces of two distinct belief systems—familial and individualistic ideologies."[2] The researchers expressed some surprise when they discovered conflicting value systems within the same woman, examples of what I call culturally acceptable values alongside the new, minority view of individualism for women. Yet most women seemed to handle the contradictions satisfactorily. They believed in women's independence and held part-time jobs while remaining committed to family and marriage. They still chauffeured their children to after-school activities, but they also spoke of their own individual needs for self-fulfillment. They are apt examples of the cafeteria women who pick and choose values, behaviors, and styles from the great assortment available to them in the infinite environment of affluent America.

The cafeteria. The image evoked is one of multiple offerings, many choices, displayed attractively for one's consumption. The cafeteria is also speedy, efficient, and reasonably priced. Americans are behaving more and more like cafeteria patrons. The structure, ideology, and form of the cafeteria have overtaken, or at least are rapidly overtaking, the American character. Along with its antecedents, the catalog and general store, the purveyors of the cafeteria mentality promise to reduce the world into manageable parts for American consumption, the highest goal of twentieth-century Americans. Everywhere one looks in modern America one sees evidence of the cafeteria mania; the university packages its courses in discrete units; Americans have successfully broken down the work process and work place, and every other place, into concrete units that can be operated efficiently. The cafeteria mentality has dominated and reshaped the physical and mental environment.

The twentieth-century cafeteria and fast-food chains express the same world view. They are the material proof of the American's belief that the universe is capable of fragmentation and specialization; furthermore, they illustrate the love of variability and variety that so characterizes the American mind. They exhibit the American's optimistic belief that the world is an infinite cafeteria with every want satisfiable, every need and craving satiable. In this sense, the cafeteria also represents the world view of Americans. The material institutions of a culture reflect its value system. The external shape of buildings and the internal functions they fulfill all express aspects of the culture. While the dichotomous view of the world (mind/body, heart/head) is well known in Western thought, the American of the late twentieth century is displaying the multiple view, the cafeteria view, of the world.

The cafeteria view is a view and a set of behavior patterns that split human experience into many small parts, with the day being divided between various work, leisure, and social activities. Americans don new identities, shed old roles, and search continuously for new and better activities with a bewildering speed. Just as the supermarket, the department store, and McDonald's package goods in small, exportable units, so Americans segment themselves into time and activity patterns that require specialized and fragmented behavior from them. Not only do Americans purchase perishable goods with fickle abandon, they buy new values, new personalities, and new clothes with the same thoughtlessness.

There is a happy marriage in America between the marketers, the primary articulators of the cafeteria approach to life, and the American people. Precisely because Americans love newness, novelty, and change, the sellers of diverse goods and services can successfully supply and profit from their insatiable appetites. Further, as I will argue in subsequent chapters, the two groups in American society most vulnerable to the marketers' messages are youths and women. Because youths and women in late twentieth-century America have the most unformed personalities, they are most susceptible to the blandishments of the marketers. The powerful allure of the cafeteria approach, moreover, is the fact that if the new fad, identity, product, or service does not please, it can easily be replaced with another, ostensibly more desirable, alternative. In the ideal cafeteria promised by the marketers, there is always another choice, another entry that can be tried, used, and discarded.

Individual identity and national identity merge at some point. The very basis of a culture is the shared traits of its participants. People gain their sense of self from an exploration of themselves within a specific cultural context. One learns about oneself, one's strengths and weaknesses, within a cultural environment of opportunity and challenge, not in a vacuum. A culture validates and punishes individual behavior. In this way, the individual's testing of self is either confirmed and supported, or denied. With the advent of the cafeteria mentality, however, the culture and individual have both succumbed to a nondiscriminatory, nonjudgmental approach to life. Everything goes; there are no limits in the infinite cafeteria.

This book is an extended essay exploring some national structural and ideological features of twentieth-century American life that have affected American personality development. The conclusion is contained within the title. These views, of course, are not uniquely mine, but I hope the following analysis, based upon a different reading of twentieth-century American life, will view the emergence of the cafeteria personality through a different perspective.

The cafeteria, I believe, is the appropriate image. It aptly captures the variety, the speed, and the often indiscriminate way Americans choose their food, their games, and their identities. Americans compartmentalize their personalities, shelving undesirable or unusable parts, while creating new dimensions to present to the public. Human personalities, American marketers and eager consumers argue, can be packaged in much the same way as hamburgers. A growing number of Americans rush to weekend therapy sessions to change themselves and to attain a new sense of self. Just as the same detergent gets a new box every few months, so an impressionable American gets a new wardrobe and hairstyle to achieve the same result—to be bought, accepted, in the marketplace. The powerful, indeed dominating, metaphor of the twentieth century in America is that of the cafeteria. It is the symbol and structure that effectively explains Americans' eternal mobility—moving from home to home, job to job, movie to movie, car to car—love of newness and devotion to change for its own sake. The cafeteria mentality, arising out of the actual cafeteria, satisfies all of these needs.

Growing up in America used to be a predictable matter. Farmers' sons and daughters could rely upon their parents' vision of their future. Surely some daring and iconoclastic people defied predictability, but most children looked forward to an adult destiny like the older generation's. They were shaped by both universal and cultural determinants of life—one's sex, color, class, and religion. Their human identities were formed within the boundaries of these essential features. Throughout history, the female child, for example, shared her adult fate with many other female children born on this planet. Black people experienced discrimination in white societies all over the world, though the nature and particular expression of the discrimination varied from culture to culture. Rich people fared considerably better than poor people in all times and places and assured their children, regardless of their abilities, a better future.

In the twentieth century, American parents and

children have found it more confusing and difficult to know who they are. Growing up has become a more unpredictable experience. Parents have had a harder time instilling traditional values in their children. Social institutions have kept changing their messages, promises made have been left unkept, and a generation, composed of people sharing attitudes, was shortened from twenty years to ten and currently to around five years. The implications for child raising, for shared cultural experiences, and for the very idea of childhood have changed.

Twentieth-century Americans, newly arrived immigrants, new city dwellers, and new factory workers all had to (and have to) face challenges to their traditional sources of identity. The material conditions of urban, industrial life created a whole new set of forces that have undermined, reshaped, and redefined the American's identity. The cultural and subcultural institutions that traditionally shaped a child's life (family, religion, work, school, and play) all have been affected by the new conditions. They have interacted with four important new by-products of twentieth-century American life—extended schooling, the generation gap, an identifiable youth culture, and effective birth-control methods.

Extended schooling, a result of the urban industrial life, has dramatically increased the power of professional educators over the lives of individuals. Most education, prior to this century, occurred in the home or the work place. Fathers taught sons all they had to learn about farming. The apprenticeship system gave boys on-the-job training in skilled and semiskilled crafts. Even lawyering and doctoring were learned in the work place. Girls learned the domestic arts from their mothers and older sisters. The few young women who went to work in textile mills in the last century learned their skills in the factory. Education was truly elementary; that is, brief, sporadic, and minimal. Only the rich could afford the luxury of allowing their children (primarily their sons) to go to school for long periods of time.

In the late nineteenth century, time in school increased, first with elementary schools becoming compulsory and then with the sudden rise of high schools; consequently, educators increased their functions and their aims. Schools became more ambitious and more self-assured. To receive more and more public dollars, educators promised more and more to their constituents. The power shifted from the family to the school. Not only were minimal literacy and basic arithmetic skills taught, but expanded time in school required expanded objectives as well. Schools became centers for preparing students for occupations and for life, two lofty goals never intended before by American schools. Classicists battled vocationalists for dominance in the early twentieth-century school.

As the connections between education and job training increased, the schools became the powerful shapers of human identity. As children created human associations based on their occupation, identity became tied, more and more, to achievement rather than to traditional ascriptive means. Who you are, who you would become, was decided in the schools. A college preparatory curriculum led the student to a predictably more desirable adult future than the vocational course of study. Many of the other identity-producing agencies of American life (most notably the family and religious institutions) lost their prominence as the educational establishment gained in power and importance.

The second new feature of twentieth-century life to radically alter the traditional ways that individuals gained a sense of self was the growing chasm between generations. The gap between parents and children was first evident in the newly arriving immigrant families but gradually became a characteristic of all American families. Immigrant parents found their skills, wisdom, and perspectives were not helpful in aiding their children to become Americans. What is more, the children looked to their new peers and teachers as well as popular cultural sources for their role models and guides to proper behavior. The parents' authority was undermined; they no longer taught their children their future occupation and their "ways" appeared Old World and undesirable to the youths striving for Americanization. As Christopher Lasch has said on this subject, "The traditional conflict of generations was reversed: the children here were the realists, the parents, idealists and dreamers, clinging to the vision of a better world."[3]

Most profoundly, the children's lives were decidedly different from their parents. Neither generation could predict the outcome. Parents looked with horror at children who openly defied them. They had no conceptual framework within which to understand the new occupations of their children, the new aspirations, and the new behavioral patterns. The gap sometimes became a chasm. As new occupations increased in twentieth-century American life and as the time in school also increased, youths spoke more to their peers than to their parents. The peer culture became a support group, a knowing cushion in the eternal struggle with uncomprehending parents. The distinctly different world views of parents and children have become even more dramatic as the century draws to a close.

Indeed, the emergence of an identifiable youth culture, age segregated and ideologically different from their parents' generation, rose inevitably from the generational conflict and became the third new factor in twentieth-century life. Youths confer identity and status upon themselves; that appears to be the most significant outcome of the blossoming of a youth culture. The youth culture may be housed in school, in leisure activities, or it may exist parallel with these other influential institutions, but its distinctiveness is apparent to all observers. The youth culture has its clothing style, its behavior style, and its value system. It may openly reject the other identity-producing agencies as anachronistic and old-fashioned or it may blithely ignore them. In either case, it became, in the last quarter of the twentieth century, a major competitor for the time, energy, spirit, and soul of a significant portion of the American population. It also appeared to preserve its hold on individuals for more and more years. Whereas the youth culture of the 1950s lost its influence on its constituents when they entered the work world at eighteen or twenty-two, the contemporary youth culture finds thirty- and forty-year-olds still identifying with it, an important new social phenomenon.

The fourth variable that has changed American life in this century has been experienced at different rates by different subgroups of Americans, a fact that pertains to the generation gap also. Birth control has brought a consciousness and a power to women's lives never before known. American women can plan their adult lives in an unprecedented way. In the early twentieth century, modern birth-control information and devices were available only for upper- and middle-class, white women. Since the 1960s, the pill has become available to all women. With family size decreasing in this century, women have had the awesome task of considering how they should spend their adult years. Early in this century, the majority continued to define themselves primarily as wives and mothers and secondarily as community volunteer workers, factory and office workers, and professionals. With smaller families, many middle-class, white women devoted themselves with even greater zeal to being a parent. The responsibility of motherhood became a time-consuming task.

Mothers read child-raising booklets in great numbers, attended child-raising classes, and joined the newly formed parent-teacher association. The fewer children were also planned with a two- or three-year interval of one another so that the period of childbearing and raising was diminished. This had many important ramifications for both the child and the mother. For the child, there were fewer older children who could point the way and ease their journey to adulthood. For the mother, each child became a more precious commodity; she had less help in raising the child, but she also had fewer household responsibilities. Consequently the job of training each child and of endowing it with a special identity increased. Position in the family also became an important new feature. In a nineteenth-century family of seven children, for example, the oldest and youngest child might have received special and differential treatment, but in all likelihood all of those in the middle were treated similarly. In a small family, with greater individual attention given to each child, the identity-formation process had to be different, more careful, and more conscious.

Surely immigrant families in 1900 and poor Southern families, both black and white, did not practice effective birth control; nor did devout Catholic families. The effect of birth control and smaller families has been experienced in each subgroup differently and at different time periods within the century. But one of the important results of the birth-control movement has been its growing effects on all segments of the population. It has affected women's consciousness about themselves as well as about their offspring. Women, the traditional mainstays of the family, have experienced identity crises as adults, a rather recent phenomenon. With more time to explore their own needs, women in the last quarter of the twentieth century are returning to college and reentering the job market *after* raising their children.

American women live longer adult lives after their last child is born and have more time to consider their life's meaning. The women's liberation movement of the late 1960s and the more general women's movement of the 1970s encouraged women to redefine themselves as individuals rather than as family members, and as women rather than as wives and mothers. Women are reentering the work force in record numbers as well as enrolling in community colleges and universities. They are restructuring the social roles within the home and creating new human arrangements for themselves and their families. In so doing, they are forging new identities, taking charge of their adult destinies in an unprecedented and dramatic fashion, and inevitably changing their relationships with their children. The home environment has been unalterably changed by the new feminism. Rather than the traditional identity-conferring agencies telling women who they are, individual women and collectivities of women are creating their own definitions.

Indeed, women and youths have emerged in the last quarter of the twentieth century as the two major segments of the society ostensibly questioning the traditional identity labels placed upon them. Their rebellion, however, is not as new or visionary as that statement may imply. School and play act as major shapers of these groups' search for identity and autonomy. Indeed, the school establishment still reigns supreme as the agent conferring respectability upon youths and women. Similarly, the growing play industry seeks the dollars and the attention of women and youths with promises to confer identity, status, happiness, and success upon them. Though the work world remains a powerful contender for their collective attention, both the family and religion are losers in this power struggle. The work world, while competing for the talents of the able young, are, at best, ambivalent about the adult returning woman. The work world would rather see women as consumers of their products than as workers in their factories and offices.

Women's awareness of themselves, the emergence of a youth subculture, the lengthening of school for all youths, and the continued conflicts between the generations all play out their themes and counterthemes in the context of the family, religion, work, school, and play. These powerful forces have absorbed some of the challenges better than others. Family, school, religion, and work, for example, have all cooperated in the growth of education into a superindustry as well as a powerful identity-forming institution. All of these networks of influences have acted in a coalitional or competitive relationship to each other throughout the century. At the beginning of the century, family and work were the dominant members of the coalition while school and play played less significant roles. As time went on, the two latter forces increased their roles.

In America a person's work remains the key to a person's identity. "What do you do for a living?" is quickly translated into "Who are you?" But the nature of human work, its demands and its rewards, has undergone dramatic changes in this century so that, at century's close, it no longer determines human identity for many people. Jobs become obsolete in a generation or less and have therefore lost their adult identity status. One's job may be temporary, not permanent, and cannot confer meaning, direction, and purpose to one's sense of self.

But the relationship between work and school remains close and collaborative. Business executives subsidize business programs in the university, sit on boards of education, and contribute substantial tax dollars to education. Schools cater to the marketplace in their curricula. Schools have gone from providing vocational training programs at the beginning of the century to undergraduate degrees in business management near the century's end. Graduate schools gather their students from workers eager to improve their job credentials. Educators have become one of the largest professions precisely because they have promised to confer human identity and adult purpose on their products. Both the family and work have a vested interest in trusting the educational establishment and in providing it with the funds it desires to carry out its purpose.

Play emerged in the last quarter of the twentieth century as a powerful force that threatens to overtake the other institutions as the dominant identity-conferring institution. With the increase in leisure time, early retirement, longer life, and an affluent youth group, more and more Americans invest more and more of their time, energy, sense of self, and money in leisure-time activities. Though much of their investment results in passive watching of commercialized productions, there is also an increase in participatory activities. While Americans danced, played the piano, and sang in 1900, they both dance and watch others dance in the 1980s. Watching television probably consumes the most time of all leisure-time activities, but the evidence suggests an increase in jogging, tennis, and other forms of participatory sports. Leisure products and facilities have become part of a major industry by the end of the century. Americans spend billions of dollars annually on amusements.

Sports have undergone significant changes within the century so that baseball, football, and basketball leagues resemble corporate conglomerates rather than informal, amateur enterprises of the nineteenth century. The recording industry enjoys new prosperity, thanks to rock n' roll music and the power of the child consumer, while movies have come and gone as a majority form of entertainment. New sporting activities, such as walking, require special shoes. Americans of all ages, but especially those between fourteen and forty, constitute a major market for the play sector of American life.

Throughout the twentieth century, the relationship between family, religion, work, school, and play has changed. The result of this complex interaction is an eclectic American, a person whose identity is formed by a variety of forces, sometimes conflicting, sometimes in harmony. The emerging American personality is a patchwork affair. There is no single, cohesive value system that governs the individual. Indeed, few seem to sense the need for consistency or cohesion. The eclectic nature of the self is more often celebrated than criticized. Consistency is no longer a virtue. Family values, religious truths, peer custom, pragmatic opportunism, and the rules of the game all intermingle in the individual personality to form an uneasy, rarely codified, whole. American personalities are becoming increasingly fickle, ever changing to changing fads, fashions, and influences of the popular culture.

The following chapters look at selective themes associated with growing up in twentieth-century America. The unusual congruence of compulsory schooling, the rise of a youth culture, and the coming of age of adult women in the 1960s have resulted in the creation of the cafeteria personality. This is a new personality type unique to growing up American in this century. Surely not all Americans fit neatly into this one generalization, but my contention is that we have all been affected by the changes in our basic identity-forming institutions. I recognize that for some of us, for example, family and religion retained their power long after it lost its preeminence for many Americans. Work, similarly, remains important for many people. But the shifts in power and importance point toward a school and play dominance as the century closes. As Americans spend less and less time in work and more and more time in school and play, these two members of the coalition exert greater influence upon the emerging eclectic American personality.

Because the emerging personality is formed from multiple, unlikely, and inconsistent sources, it often has an unfinished quality to it. This is understandable since the identity-forming institutions themselves are not sure of their purpose, role, or destiny. They too change their messages frequently. The family has lost its moorings, school revamps its programs regularly in a desperate attempt to become effective, work must interest an apathetic generation, and play becomes more and more daring in its grab for American followers. All forces continue to influence and shape the American personality but the tug-of-war has no rationality to it, few collaborative threads, and little understanding of its cross purposes. The family has begun to doubt the value of school, the work world criticizes the school's graduates, and play advocates preach a value system antithetical to both the work and family values. The traditional collaborations are breaking down with no single force having the power to confer new sources of identity.

The following chapters knowingly operate at a very high level of generalization. Further, each chapter organizes the historical experience within this idiosyncratic perspective and selects specific themes and moments to describe the relationship between the identity-conferring agencies. Americans acted as both victims and actors in the power struggle over their lives and fates. They followed the lead of both traditional and new guides to human conduct. They accepted different answers to the same questions during the century and willingly tried each new institutional approach to their problems. Their paths reflected their cultural values. Because Americans value practical knowledge, for example, they voluntarily followed school experts, child-raising experts, and work experts who told them what they had to do to lead a successful adult life in America. In the last quarter of the century, they follow mental health experts in search for self.

With the improved communications of the post–World War II period, growing up is done within a much larger perspective than that of an isolated farming community of 1845. Television, particularly, has transformed the cultural environment within which children grow up. Rural and urban, black and white, rich and poor share the same morning, afternoon, and evening television schedule. They share a vocabulary, a common vision of reality, and a common set of fantasies. The manufactured culture of television creates a national child personality unlike anything previously experienced in American history. As already suggested, school and play have become the determining variables for growing up in America today. Within the play mode, television dominates.

Cafeteria America offers historical and contemporary analyses of some of the key themes of our twentieth-century experience. They are given as suggestive probings into the ingredients that compose the contemporary ethos and the dominant personality type. The following chapters touch the general features of the growing up experience rather than the concrete texture of it; they provide frameworks within which much additional research and writing can be done. The experiences of American women, as children and adults, frequently become the primary symbols and evidences for the points being made throughout this book; the female experience of growing up in America, the making of American women into the ultimate cafeteria personalities, constitutes a major theme.

Chapter

2

Generational Agreements and Disagreements

Throughout human history, parents and children have clashed on the fundamental question of authority. Adolescent children, particularly, challenge the wisdom, experience, and authority of their parents; they assert their right to independence and independent decision making. In most societies prior to the nineteenth century, the children's rebellion gave way to acceptance of parental authority. This occurred for psychological and socially pragmatic reasons. Once adolescents tested their power and began to understand their boundaries, they learned to operate within self-defined and socially defined limits. Further, they learned that the parent's wisdom was indeed useful in making the transition into the adult world. Children often learned their adult skills from their parents and thus found that the parent was their employer, teacher, and guide. Children lived and worked in close proximity to their parents, shared all life's experiences with them, and identified as members of the family unit even after they began their own family.

The industrial and urban revolutions changed this human scenario drastically, especially for the growing middle class. Indeed, the middle class came into existence as a major class precisely because of the industrial revolution. Sons and daughters of skilled workers and small entrepreneurs became white-collar workers in the new offices and the teachers and professionals in the new cities. The children of the middle class lived lives distinctly different from their parents. They learned occupations that were unheard of in their parents' generation. They moved their homes away from their parents; they engaged in leisure-time activities unknown to their parents, and they prepared their children for middle-class lives by teaching them the virtues of independence, self-discipline, and decision making.

In so doing, they sowed the seeds of generational conflict. Different occupations of father and son do not inherently create generational problems; however, the upward mobility and increased ambition of the new middle-class member leads to different living patterns, a desire to better oneself, and an identification of the parental generation as old-fashioned, traditional, and backward. In a society where newness and novelty are valued goals, parents are identified with the old and the traditional. Further, everyone can see the dramatic differences in attitudes, work opportunities, and educational achievements between the generations. There are now appreciable contrasts, not just harmonious continuities, between the generations.

In contrast, urban working-class families and farming families remained closely knit units for a longer time, with strong loyalties to kin, precisely because the children continued to prepare for the same adult life as the parents. The middle-class family became more isolated, more independent, and unwittingly more estranged from its children. By training children to be on their own, to train for new and ambitious life roles, and to think for themselves, parents created the conflicts between the generations that often became permanent chasms. By acknowledging that the different occupational future of the children required a different world view, parents sanctioned the separation between the generations. Parents also, by abdicating their authority, opened the way for their children to develop cafeteria personalities, morally and culturally ungrounded personalities that pick and choose mates, occupations, and pleasures throughout life.

Without clear guidelines, all options take on equal value. So as parents relinquished control over their children's futures, so the myriad of life and job choices presented themselves as equal in worth and importance. Schools pursued the cafeteria mentality with a vengeance while the family, the only other logical anchor in an increasingly anchorless world, abdicated their responsibility to the experts. Parents were beguiled and deceived by the American love of variety and infinite possibility for the future and for their children's future. The experts and marketers of modern America compartmentalized life, identity, and knowledge and packaged humans as any other product. The most convincing sales presentation won out over all other contenders.

While all families experienced temporary adolescent rebellion, it was the middle-class family that first experienced serious, chronic problems of communication and the weakening of family loyalties. Parents became unsure of themselves and of their authority because they no longer trained their children for adulthood. They had lost the fundamental role that tied the generations together. The city, the public schools, competing philosophies, and the new work world created bewildered parents who no longer looked with confidence upon their progeny. Everyone looked to the experts for guidance in each specialized human task and stage of development.

It is in the twentieth century that the full effects of the industrial revolution became apparent to urban Americans. As a result, at least two features of the industrializing process developed that had tremendous consequences for the cafeteria mentality: (1) the production of surplus goods necessitating consumers to buy with a regularity and intensity unknown to human history, and (2) the weakening of ties between generations as children learned new occupational skills for the ever-changing industrial world.

Randolph Bourne, an astute social commentator in the early part of this century, dealt with some of these very same issues in a 1911 essay he wrote for *Atlantic Monthly* called "The Two Generations." "Parents frankly do not understand their children, and their lack of understanding and of control over them means a lack of the moral guidance which, it has always been assumed, young people need until they are safely launched in the world."[1] Bourne then directed his attention to the coming generation and its characteristics. The picture he drew was of a world without clear guidelines so that youth growing up early in the century could not rely upon any authority figure. The new features of the work world, and of the preparatory educational world, played the major roles in creating this confusing and guideless environment.

Bourne proved to be prophetic in his appraisal of the relationship between the generations. He sensed that the twentieth century offered new opportunities, challenges, and problems that widened the gap between the generations. "It must be remembered that we of the rising generation have to work this problem out all alone. Pastors, teachers, and parents flutter aimlessly about with their ready-made formulas, but somehow these are less efficacious than they used to be. I doubt if any generation was ever thrown quite so completely on its own resources as ours is."[2] Bourne sensed a loss of confidence on the part of parents and all elders and the need for the young to solve their own problems. This tendency, of the parents to relinquish authority and control over their children, would become more and more apparent as the century continued.

Bourne concluded optimistically however. He believed that the younger generation would find its way, with some help from its elders, but the reader in the 1980s may not share Bourne's optimism. His discussion of the failure of parents to provide moral guidance strikes at the heart of my thesis; since parents in the preindustrial world knew confidently what their children's adult futures would be, they could provide rules and advice in every area of life; they could participate confidently in the shaping of their children's identity. Their ethics, their work, their community would all be their children's. They shared a universe and they actively created their children's adult personality and future. Thus, the traditional adolescent rebellion was a temporary phase, one that did not jeopardize anyone's adult future. But in the new industrial, urban world, parents would not know with any sureness what the child's future would be like. Thus, they wavered in counseling their children in all areas, in their schooling, in their religious training, and in their future plans.

It was precisely at this point that the wavering parents confronted the growing numbers of experts. Middle-class members are the first to succumb to the temptation of using an expert. They are impressed by the credentials of the experts, as are most Americans, especially if the experts promise concrete and practical rewards for engaging their services. The growing reliance on experts in all areas of human life acknowledges individuals' confusion and lack of confidence in their own judgment. With the profusion of information and its dissemination through communications technology, newly arriving city folk find themselves faced with specialists in all areas eager to inform them, to guide them, to consult with them, and to lead them. Specialization of labor and knowledge emerges as an integral part of the new industrial and urban age; universities in the twentieth century expand their departments, their specialties, and their services as does industry. Eventually, an imperialism of specialties overwhelms all phases of life so that child-raising experts, be they psychologists, guidance counselors, pediatricians, or education professors, all vie for the attention and money of their growing clientele. The public becomes a market, a constituency for the growing numbers of experts in all areas.

This phenomenon dramatized not only generational differences and created more differentiated socioeconomic classes, but it also heightened the view of the older person (the expert) explaining the world to the younger (the next generation). Moreover, as knowledge increased and became more complex, it took longer and longer to explain the new world to the younger generation. While fathers could teach sons farming tasks in a rather short time and practice was the primary teacher, in a world of expertise, courses of study grow longer and longer, and the younger generation remain dependent upon the expert generation for extended periods.

Science and technology claim many virtues and rewards for those who follow its ways; scientists and technicians speak the truth, a truth scientifically proven, and they use efficient and objective methods to accomplish their aims. Neither custom, past experience, nor family traditions can stand up in the face of formidable science. Thus, middle-class parents, anxious to be modern, embraced the scientific method and its practitioners. They used experts, be they doctors, therapists, or teachers, to counsel them in the proper ways of raising their children and in preparing them for a scientifically advancing society.

Mothers-to-be started using the new, modern hospital to have their babies. Child-raising books increased in popularity. Parents now conferred with others in the practice of child raising, an activity that had always been accomplished by the parents, possibly with the aid of other family members and intimates, but not with outsiders. Children, in this new environment, observed the fallibility of their parents; answers for sometimes obvious questions were asked of experts and solemn discussions ensued; and the process that began early in the century and has only accelerated since, took on a seemingly unstoppable momentum.

The concept of generation is more amorphous and less easily definable today than ever before. When sociologists first began conceptualizing on the subject in the late nineteenth century, they defined a generation as an age group that had shared a major transforming event such as war or revolution, an event that separated that age group from all others. Usually the idea would apply to a twenty-year collectivity. Eighteen-year-olds to thirty-eight-year-olds experienced revolution in much the same way, according to this thesis. As the twentieth century has continued, the age of a generation has shortened; some people argue today that a high school freshman and a college senior no longer speak the same language or share the same outlook. Others argue that though there has been segmentation within a generation, the concept and its age characteristics still have meaning.

French sociologist Annie Kriegel has argued, in a provocative essay called "Generational Difference: The History of an Idea," that there is usually more continuity than difference between the generations. However, she acknowledges that there are differences. Kriegel posits the thesis that in each generation there are three responses to a major social event: (1) the very few for whom the event transforms their lives, (2) a greater number for whom the event is influential and important but not determining, (3) and the vast majority for whom the event is irrelevant or unnoticed. One could modify this model to suggests that external conditions influence everyone in differing ways and that the integrating ability of humans is such that the old and the new can be merged in multiple and unpredictable ways.

In the late twentieth century, for example, Americans are living longer than ever before. Improved health conditions have extended life expectancy in dramatic ways. This fact affects all generations and all members of each generation, though the way it affects them and the way individuals within each generation act on this fact may vary. Some sixty-year-olds will look forward to a longer work life; many will retire early and look forward to a leisurely retirement; some will begin new personal relationships; and still others will be unable to adapt mentally to life's new possibilities. Similarly, the 1960s youth generation, then and since, have not all behaved identically. All college students, indeed most college students in 1964, did not demonstrate against the war in Vietnam; most did not reject their parents' values; and most continued on the regular life course as expected. But many absorbed the ideology of liberation and emancipation in some parts of their lives, particularly in their sexual practices and in their devotion to personal pleasure.

The definition of generation, historically, has changed during this century. So have the social realities. Kriegel claims that World War II was the last major event of this century and that most social change since has been fads and fashions, ephemeral things. Whether the generation growing up after 1945 consciously thought about the prospect of nuclear destruction, as some have claimed, is uncertain, but surely Kriegel's model is useful in analyzing a generation's response to atomic energy. In the early 1980s, a worldwide nuclear disarmament movement began, an effort to alert world citizenry to the danger of nuclear warfare. Whether this period of multiple generations, each with its own history, will respond, or how it will respond, remains to be seen.

This may be the first time in human history when so many generations coexist. There are Americans alive today who grew up during World War I and were mature adults at the time of the Great Depression. As the population ages, and also lives longer, multiple generations, each with different growing-up experiences will mingle and, it is hoped, cooperate. Because the material conditions of American life have changed so dramatically in this century (indeed the eighty-year-old today remembers horse-drawn carriages, while having learned how to use a library computer terminal) the past as authority loses its hold for everyone. Not only do parents question their ability to govern their children, but all members of all generations question their own wisdom about many things. They all witness so many changes in the bewildering cafeteria of America that it is hard to rely on past knowledge or experience for present problems.

Along with the middle class, the first modernizing class in this century, immigrants also faced the problem of generational conflict. Early in the century, the newly arriving eastern and southern European children, raised in the strange, new American culture, quickly identified with it against the Old World culture of their parents. In the 1970s and 1980s, newly arriving immigrants from Asia, Mexico, and Latin America faced the same problem. Indeed, the causes of the generational conflict were the same: the children faced an uncertain and decidedly different future from that of their parents. The immigrant children positively sought the different future in contrast to the middle-class children whose changed circumstances dictated their actions. But in both cases, the parents no longer participated actively in the shaping of the children's identity and adult future. Immigrant parents were bewildered by the new America and clung to their traditional ways; middle-class parents tried to prepare their children for an uncertain future by teaching them the very qualities that would lead to a split between the generations. The rugged individualism of frontier America was always coupled with a sense of community and cooperation. In urban, industrial America, the fierce competitive spirit reappeared, but it focused almost entirely on the individual with little regard for that sense of community and cooperation.

The ties between the generations are many: affection, loyalty, duty, and a shared world view. In some families, all the links remain strong and attached; in most, some are weakened and/or broken. When the shared world view is lost, both generations find it tense and frustrating to maintain affectionate relations. If parents and children disagree about the meaning of personal behavior and what the future will bring, the relationship is seriously endangered. Elizabeth Stern, daughter of immigrants, described the shattering of her family's world view in her memoir *My Mother and I*.[3] Stern told of her rabbi father's difficulties in earning a living and her remembrances of a hard-working mother who tried in vain to provide for the four children. Elizabeth wanted to go to high school, an unprecedented action in her neighborhood. Her father disapproved, arguing that it would alienate her from her family and her religion. Her mother supported her wish to better herself.

Elizabeth went to high school, the only girl from her elementary school to do so. Her father's prophecy was accurate; she went on to college, moved to New York, and rarely saw her family. Eventually she married a Christian and erased all her ties to Judaism and her Jewish family. The contrast between a religiously orthodox parent and a disbelieving child provides a dramatic example of generational conflict. The absolutism of the father could not be compromised or beat; the daughter was required to accept or reject the total faith. Elizabeth Stern chose rejection.

Elizabeth Stern's experience of separation from her family was feared by all immigrant parents. But the conflict was inherent and insoluble; most parents were not religiously orthodox and they sought to aid their children in their quest for educational and economic success in America. By pursuing these goals, however, they often broke the ties of a shared world view and affection. If the parents pushed their children, eager to see them succeed, they often alienated the exasperated children; if the children succeeded, they complimented themselves upon their accomplishment and blushed when their parents took credit for their success. In either case, the ties between the generation became strained.

In a fictional example of generational conflict, "The Gold in Fish," Fannie Hurst describes how successful son Morris comes to his parents' home one day to tell them he is changing the family name of Goldfish to Fish. Both parents are bewildered and resistant. The mother comments, "You hear that, papa. The name that was good enough for you to get born into, and for me to marry into, is something to be ashamed of."[4] Only one daughter, Birdie, sympathizes with her parents and unsuccessfully tries to convince Morris that the family name is fine. Later, when her father is on his deathbed, Birdie tells her brother Morris that his generous financial support of his parents has deprived them of their culture, their tastes, and their activities.

That's what they are. Two Goldfish out of water. I know them! I know every time ma puts a hat on her head it gives her a headache. I know how she goes on the sly and buys herself a miltz and sneaks in the kitchen on the cook's day out to fix it for her and pa. I know how pa'd rather haggle selling a secondhand, golden-pak roller-tip Grand Rapids desk to Jacob Mintz than sit sunning himself all day in a Heppel-white chair, that he cannot pronounce.[5]

Birdie never convinces Morris of the authenticity of their parents' lives and culture. The father dies and Birdie takes her mother to live with her in her home. Except for one compassionate child, the communication between the generations ended.

Immigrant and native daughters had a particular struggle in the generational war. Being girls, they were expected to be obedient and submissive to the parental will. Even in aspiring, mobile middle-class homes, daughters were not expected to obtain as much education as sons; their adult roles were predetermined for them. All girls grew up to become wives and mothers, adult roles that could be taught by their mothers. So while the intergenerational conflict was played out between parents and sons, daughters who sought advanced education and public lives other than wife, mother, or volunteer were especially punished if they challenged parental authority. Fathers and sons often reconciled and overcame their differences; estranged daughters had a harder time.

The core of the issue was identity. Parents, as representatives of the larger culture, had always conferred identity upon their children. They invested them with religious values, social rules, and occupational skills. They acted as society's agent in preparing the next generation for life in the larger culture. By removing those functions from the home, by allowing the school and the work world to define the individual, the major characteristics of industrial and urban living in the twentieth century, the family lost its essential relationship to the young. It no longer conferred identity. Its authority had been stolen away from it. The generational ties were reduced to affection, duty, and loyalty. And on some occasions, guilt. None of these ties were as powerful and sure as when both generations shared a world view with the parents acting as teachers and guides.

In the essay "The Crisis in Education," written in the 1950s, philosopher Hannah Arendt discussed the general loss of authority in the modern world. While all social forces seemed unable to cope with the bewildering changes of modern society, she described parents' attitudes toward their children: "In this world even we are not very securely at home; how to move about in it, what to know, what skills to master, are mysteries to us too. You must try to make out as best you can; in any case you are not entitled to call us to account. We are innocent, we wash our hands of you."[6]

In this analysis, both generations, parents and children alike, seem eager to renounce responsibility toward one another. Elizabeth Stern justified her break with her family as necessary for her individual maturation and liberation, while the mythic parents described by Arendt deny the ability to guide their children in the world's ways. In both cases, the traditional generational conflict has deteriorated to a nonrelationship. The condition that Bourne prophesied early in the century was repeated by Arendt over forty years later.

Working-class families avoided these generational conflicts as long as the work of parents and children remained roughly equivalent and while religious and cultural ties continued to be strong. Sociologists do not necessarily share my thesis; they disagree among themselves as to whether working-class people identify with middle-class values or whether they possess distinctive values that keep them separate from middle-class culture. Another possibility, of course, argued by some sociologists, is that the members of an ethnic working-class group are participants in both their own subculture and in the mainstream culture. In my view, the significant variables to be considered are the two generations' world view and their work. While some working-class groups display family cohesiveness unknown to the middle class, the ambitious and socially mobile members of the working class often behave like the middle class; they abandon the extended family culture in favor of a nuclear, isolated family. The links between the generations become weakened in these families.[7]

If American life is becoming more and more homogenized, as many social commentators argue, and if class distinctions blur still further, working-class subcultures are destined to experience the same generational conflicts known to immigrants and the middle class. Family ties based on tradition, respect, authority, and intergenerational conviviality will disappear from all subcultural group behavior, be it working class or middle class. Evidence on child-raising practices suggests that working-class mothers are using the same techniques as middle-class mothers. They are relying, in increasing numbers, on experts rather than the rod.[8] This trend suggests that working-class mothers are no longer sure of themselves and of the traditional ways of child raising. They are becoming "modern" by relinquishing their mother's advice (an example of generational ties weakening) and their own common sense and experience.

In the past, the essential conflict between the generations usually worked itself out during the child's adolescent years. Adolescents rebelled against their parents' strictures in an attempt to define their own boundaries, to know who they are, what their competencies, likes, and dislikes are. With the resolution of this conflict, the two generations could live reasonably amicably side by side. As noted, the rise of middle-class urban and industrial life has created a perpetual struggle between the generations, with neither side understanding or caring to understand the other. The ties have often been severed with neither side trying to mend them.

According to this analysis, parents have contributed to the development of the cafeteria personality among their children. Immigrant and middle-class parents alike acknowledged their impotence to judge and evaluate their children's behaviors since the future seemed so different to them. Parents mistakenly assumed that since they could no longer supervise their children's education and adult occupations, they could no longer exert authority over them. They abdicated their role to the outside experts and in so doing, gave the children over to the specialists who each claimed competence in only one part of life. Dividing up a person into segments is a significant manifestation of the cafeteria mentality. All parts have equal and interchangeable value, equal meaning, and possibly no worth at all. The major guiding principle replacing tradition and parental wisdom is personal feelings, an unpredictable and unsafe basis for making important decisions.

The whole subject of generational agreements and disagreements is extremely important in considering growing up in America in any time period. Simply viewing much historical data from this perspective gives the reader a new awareness, a new way to analyze the material. In what ways are the leaders of each generation articulating the values of their parents, contemporary values, or new mergers? How original, traditional, consensual, or synthetic are the solutions offered at each period in history? What ideas are school children being given? What relationship do those ideas have to universal needs and to the particular problems of the age? These are only some of the questions evoked from the subject of generations in the context of growing up.

Another important consideration is gender differences. As already suggested, girls have traditionally been raised differently from boys. For women, marriage and motherhood have been consistently advocated, while boys have been raised with more variability and flexibility. Has this changed for young women in America and, if so, when? What roles do class and race play as well? Upper- and middle-class families educated their daughters before the working class had the means or the attitudinal change to do so, but what has that meant in terms of generational relationships? Has it increased tensions as the dutiful daughter finds that even with her refined education her parents decide upon her mate, or surely expect her to fulfill their hopes and marry after graduating from college? Are the tensions and guilt between the generations greater for women than men precisely because females are taught to be obedient and then, with new educational opportunities, trained to be rebellious?

On the psychic level, are the anxieties of the children expressed differently? Do girls struggle with mother more than father while boys struggle with father more than mother? Are there consistent patterns that can be detected based upon cultural values, religious attitudes, and class/race considerations? Imaginative literature surely can be useful in answering some of these questions, though an interrelated, and exceedingly difficult one to negotiate intrudes: how do you distinguish universal tensions and struggles from particular ones arising from a particular cultural context? In what ways do members of the same generation communicate their allegedly shared distresses? Is popular music a communicator of confirmed attitudes or a creator of them?

Multigenerational social movements also have to be examined in any consideration of generations. How does one explain organizations with member from disparate religious and social backgrounds and from every age group? Is this an instance where the universal and the particular merge? Surely the phenomenon of professionalization, an offshoot of the rise of the expert, contributes to the answer. University professors of all ages, both sexes, and differing backgrounds meet on common ground as do insurance agents, computer specialists, and restaurant owners. Occupations and interests unite people of different generations and backgrounds. In looking at reform organizations, however, it is ideology and not economic interest that binds people together. Young and old alike joined hands in the women's suffrage, civil rights, anti–Vietnam War, and nuclear disarmament struggles.

Thus, we are faced with many reasons for generational agreements and disagreements, for bridges across the generations as well as chasms. Evaluating the nature of the agreements and disagreements is one way of determining the value system of a culture. If the agreements on fundamental survival and moral issues exceed the disagreements, the culture is healthy; if the disagreements are only on stylistic and fashionable concerns, the society is not threatened. But if the opposite is true in both cases, the culture's health is in peril.

The new disagreements between the generations arising in this century, due largely to external circumstances, became one of the factors that contributed to the cafeteria mentality. Since the past, represented by the parental generation, no longer provided the only or the major way for children to live their adult lives, new and often unforeseen possibilities lay ahead for youths. Choices and uncertainties replaced the certainties of the past. Future opportunities, combined with present challenges, widened the gap between generations. Families, as traditional and vital allies in the course of a lifetime, have lost their central place in the emotional, intellectual, and recreational life of many young cafeteria Americans.

Chapter

3

Compulsory Schooling

In 1913, Chicago factory inspector Helen Todd asked over 800 children working in factories why they worked. In 381 cases, the death or sickness of the father was the reason given, an expected finding. For 269 children, one reason they preferred the factory to school was that they were not hit there. In an earlier study, the overwhelming majority of children questioned said that, if given a choice, they would prefer work to school. Some of their reasons were: "Because you get paid for what you do in a factory." "You never understand what they tells you in school, and you can learn right off to do things in a factory." "They ain't always picking on you because you don't know things in a factory." "You can go to the nickel show." "They're good to you at home when you earn money."[1]

Compulsory schooling was not yet an accepted feature of American public education. It was the combination of the abolition of child labor and compulsory school attendance laws in the early part of the twentieth century that served notice on the children of America that they were expected to attend school, not work or play in the streets. It is a forgotten feature of twentieth-century life that this message was greeted with reluctance first, followed by gradual acceptance. With the Great Depression of the 1930s, children and youths came to attend school for longer periods out of necessity—there was nowhere else to go. By the post–World War II period, few people remembered the time when the majority of thirteen- and fourteen-year-olds worked. What began as a practical response to a temporary economic catastrophe became a permanent feature of American life.

Public education has been an established part of American life since the first English colonies were organized. However, the commitment was to the limited and very practical educational goals of basic literacy, so that children could read the Bible, and basic arithmetic, so they could count. Little else was expected and little else occurred in the modest schoolrooms of America. But as the nation industrialized, the need for better educated workers and managers became apparent. Bookkeepers who could do more than count, supervisors who could write reports, and workers who could read instructions became essential to the emerging, complex society.

More years in school as well as longer school years became the cry from many quarters. Indeed, multiple agencies in our culture combined to extend public schooling. The major identity-conferring networks (the family, work, and school) all cooperated and supported the extension of education, though often for different reasons. But even when they had competing interests, as will be shown later, they ultimately cooperated for the expansion of schooling. Many immigrant parents, for example, encouraged their children to attend school so that their future would be brighter than their parents, but some ethnic groups relied on their children's labor to survive. South Italian parents needed the income from their children's labor and were not as supportive of the schools as Jewish parents were.[2] Business executives in Chicago in 1890 started a private vocational training high school to prepare students for the work world when the school system failed to act quickly enough. The growing group of professional educators encouraged school attendance for all children.

Requiring young people to go to school for extended periods of time may be the most significant social factor in the development of twentieth-century American lives. While the increase in elementary schooling was largely based upon the great influx of immigrants that required educating, the expansion of high schooling for all Americans is directly related to the Great Depression. Pragmatic and idealistic arguments were proposed in the early twentieth century, and continue to be offered, as explanations and justifications for compulsory schooling, but it was the lack of jobs for the fifteen- to eighteen-year-old population that insured their attendance in schools. The fluidity and variety of options that once characterized the educational situation has been largely replaced by a resigned acceptance of compulsory schooling as a necessary evil. By reviewing some of the past history of compulsory schooling we can see how the spectacular growth of this institution both reflected the weakening of traditional forms of identity building and contributed to the burgeoning of the cafeteria personality.

Historian David Tyack has noted that in the early years of the century "72 percent of second generation children and 69 percent of foreign born children aged 5–14 were in school in comparison with 65 percent of native children."[3] Indeed, the dramatic upsurge in the immigrant population in the urban areas of the country required the attention of educators, public officials, and industrialists. Though the factories absorbed the labor of many children, many attended school; further, the critics of child labor were instrumental in legislating compulsory school laws and child labor laws. Eventually, big business and professional educators, recognizing their mutual self-interest, collaborated to improve the school system and model it after an efficient business.

The growth of public schooling, first elementary and then high school and college in this century, is a classic case of growth justifying further growth. It was argued that each expansion of enrollment necessitated a growth in facilities, staff, and finances. Integral to the physical expansion of school and school facilities was the expansion of goals and promises to the taxpayers, who sometimes wondered whether the increase in school costs truly resulted in an increase in benefits. Professional educators invented new specialties and subspecialties, new educational positions, and new vocabulary to assure their constituents they were serving their clientele effectively and efficiently. The growth continued, so that the education industry (indeed it has begun to resemble an industry) was a 100 billion dollar enterprise by 1980.

The eventual collaboration between business and professional educators was not accomplished in a conspiratorial manner; nor was the expansion of educational specialties, terminologies, and courses. Rather, it was based on pragmatic considerations as well as the constantly expanding field of knowledge called education. Psychology, an allied field, also contributed new ideas and new words to the fascinating subject of children's education. Business groups and civic organizations often combined to study the public schools and to offer recommendations for improvement. All parties benefitted; it was a classic example of mutual benefit.[4]

Three hundred thousand children entered the New York public schools between 1899 and 1914, a 60 percent increase over 1898. By 1908, over 70 percent of the children in the New York schools were foreign born.[5] Though the dramatic increase in foreign-born students introduced new educational problems for the professionals to face and solve, they seized the challenge and presented a confident face to their public. New York City, the home of millions of new immigrants, found their situation duplicated in many other big cities. Simultaneously, American school systems were undergoing a process of modernization. With strong leadership from university presidents and deans of schools of education, school boards changed from being composed of political ward representatives to mayoral appointees from the community; the board became smaller and centralized and was led by a professional superintendent.

During the thirty-year period from 1890 to 1920, public universities and teachers colleges grew in size and offered their students courses and degrees in professional education. Colleges of education within the university spawned new courses in administration and curriculum development. The growth of a new professional class of educators, responding to the growth in the school-age population, helped to expand the school enterprise. The move toward centralization, professionalization, and bureaucratization, all phenomena labeled as late twentieth-century evils, were viewed in the years between 1890 and 1920 as progressive and desirable reforms.[6]

The cooperative interaction of family, work, and school was very evident in the growth of public schools. Immigrant and native parents were told that formal education was essential in the new industrial world; business executives, whose tax dollars supported the schools and who hired its products, dominated boards of education and imposed their views of business upon the schools; and professional educators, eager to confer respectability and importance upon themselves, promised parents and business that increased educational funding would insure personal and economic success for everyone concerned.

The spectacular twentieth-century growth of public

education was truly a collaborative effort with all major identity-conferring networks participating in its growth. As the funding increased, so did the educators' promises. Students were assured of better jobs and better adult lives if they remained in school; business was promised better workers and better citizens; and parents were told that their children could look forward to brighter futures than they had had if they graduated from elementary, or later, high school. The increased enrollment of school-age children testified to the success of the educators' message and the shared values of all concerned.

City children now attended self-contained classrooms with teachers who had some advanced schooling. The cost of education kept increasing as more and more students went to school longer. New schools had to be built in unprecedented numbers, additional teaching staff had to be hired, and superintendents needed assistants and associates to aid them in planning curricula, developing budgets, and performing administrative functions. New York City spent over 11 million dollars to run its schools in 1899; it took over 37 million dollars to perform that task in 1914. Fourteen new high schools were built during that period. Each major American city went through a similar process. Chicago's Board of Education streamlined its membership in 1917 from twenty-one members to eleven. Similarly, as early as 1892, it passed a law requiring all children under thirteen to attend school.[7]

Compulsory schooling was not easily accepted. In 1902, fifty-five New York truant officers investigated over 100,000 cases and discovered that only 670 were violations of the child labor law. Large numbers of young people simply did not want to go to school. Statistics on truancy in the early years of this century are notoriously inaccurate because teachers and administrators rarely reported authentic numbers. A high truancy rate reflected badly upon the school. Further, the additional paperwork for a teacher with fifty students was unwelcome. Indeed, a high absentee rate in such a large classroom was greeted positively by all participants.[8] There is some evidence to suggest that this situation remains essentially the same in the early 1980s. Schools do not report accurate truancy statistics nor do they report acts of student violence for fear of the negative comment upon their professional competence.

During the first two decades of this century, work and play appealed to many of America's children far more than the schools' rigid and overcrowded environment. The working children interviewed by Helen Todd questioned the worth of formal education and experienced greater immediate satisfaction from learning gained on the job; they felt better about themselves as wage earners rather than as learners. But all of society's influential groups agreed that education should be compulsory and that the school was the appropriate setting. Industrialists, business executives, reformers, educators, and parents all agreed that young people needed civilizing, Americanizing, and learning for life. Each interested constituency articulated its position and though not all scored victories on every issue, most emerged from the schooling controversy as winners. Perhaps the children were the only losers.

While I would not suggest that child labor was a blessing, I wonder whether it was the unmitigated curse that reformers said it was. Surely low wages, long hours, and deplorable working conditions required correction (for adult workers as well as children), but many of the children's comments about work made uncommon good sense. "You can learn right off to do things in a factory" may be a very intelligent approach to learning, a method that, at least according to the children, was not employed in the schoolroom. The children had a sense of pride and accomplishment from working that was reflected in better treatment by their parents, who also showed them renewed respect. "You can go to the nickel show" displayed the child's pleasure in choosing his or her own recreation and in earning money for amusement purposes. Cultivating self-worth, pride in accomplishment, and decision-making ability are surely important educational goals; perhaps the factories fulfilled those goals more readily in the early part of the century than did the schools with their rigid disciplinary methods, traditional curricula, and fanatical emphasis upon conformity and decorum.

Industrialists and business executives sought an active role in shaping school decisions because of their frustration with employing elementary school graduates who were unprepared for the business world. Their pragmatic, antihumanistic emphasis clashed with at least two other influential groups who participated in shaping school curricula. The classicists, often represented by university presidents and professors, insisted that all children, urban and rural, learn Latin and Greek, while unhappy business executives claimed a strong vocational and manual training program should be offered to the students. Experimental and progressive educators argued for a more flexible curriculum that responded to the students' needs while moralists complained about the lack of discipline in the classroom. Within each interest group, you often had representatives of both the traditional and innovative viewpoints.

The professional organization, the National Education Association, created a Committee of Ten to study the secondary education curriculum; its report of 1894 defined nine academic areas as essential to high school programs. Rather than require Latin and Greek, for example, students could now choose the areas of study as long as they fulfilled the numerical requirement of periods of study. While Latin and Greek remained two of the nine areas of study, they were no longer required of all students. This report, used as a model in many high school systems, was termed a compromise by most observers. The classicists retained a place in the academic scheme while innovators won a point for flexibility and variety of programming.

Another example of conflicting views about the nature of education was the struggle between industry and labor on vocational training. Organized labor looked upon vocational education as a way of giving industry cheap, submissive workers trained to be obedient and industrious. Industry argued that young people were inadequately trained for the modern factory and the school was required to provide them with usable skills. In Chicago, for example, a bitter struggle went on early in the century over this issue. The Cooley Bill, named after a former superintendent who advocated a two-track educational system, failed to pass the Illinois legislature in 1913, 1915, and 1917. Critics of the Cooley Bill, such as reformer-educator Superintendent Ella Flagg Young argued that a two-track educational system would keep working-class youth in their depressed condition for life; Young and her supporters were able to marshall sufficient forces to defeat the bill, but separate vocational training high schools did become part of the educational scheme. Elementary schools remained general in their curricula with no segregation according to future occupation or career goal.

In this case, as in the debate over the classics, the only clear victor was the educational establishment. Otherwise, industrialists won partial victories as did labor unions. Parents were not always sure that their children were receiving an adequate education, but they vaguely believed in the worth of education nonetheless. Business executives continued to sit on school boards and measure progress in their terms. Modie J. Spiegel, chairman of the Finance Committee of the Chicago Board of Education in 1912, told a Child Welfare Conference that the Chicago schools were improving. His standard of measurement was the number of children in a classroom and the number of classrooms in the city. Since he joined the School Board, he declared, the classroom size had decreased from sixty students per class to forty-five. He confidently concluded that with additional money, the number would be reduced still further and truancy would be eliminated as a problem.[9]

Marvin Lazerson and W. Norton Grubb argued in their

study of American education and vocationalism that though vocational education did not become the widespread educational model its advocates desired, the concept of vocationalism profoundly affected American education.[10] As a result of the vocational education debate in the pre–World War I period, the high school became the setting for job-training courses and, more importantly, for the equation of education and vocational training. Further, the previous goal of education as moral training for all American youth was replaced with vocational guidance testing and separate curricula for different ability levels and social classes. Thus, to Lazerson and Grubb, the introduction of the concept of vocationalism drastically altered the vision of schooling; upper-class youth were tracked into college preparatory courses while working-class children were directed to manual arts classes.

The public discussion about vocational education most likely reflected the new socioeconomic reality for urban Americans. By 1914, most American children went to elementary school. When they dropped out to work at the age of twelve or thirteen, they were told that their future job opportunities would be severely restricted because of their limited education. The growing industrial society required skilled and literate workers and doomed the unskilled and uneducated to perpetual poverty. As self-made businessmen and entrepreneurial opportunities decreased, the cry for more and more practically oriented schooling increased. As more and more children went to school, taxpayers demanded concrete evidence that their dollars were well spent. Claiming the teaching of practical skills was surely one way of placating the schools' critics. Finally, by discussing vocationalism within the context of the school, the equation of education equaling job preparation was proposed and confirmed for the first time in American educational history.

With the sealing of this new equation, American schools had replaced the first and major reason for education, moral teachings, with the more practical and concrete goal of vocational preparation. Alongside citizenship training, especially necessary for the growing numbers of immigrant children in the urban elementary schools, American parents and children came to expect the schools to prepare youth for their adult life's work. It would be a logical step, as the educational establishment grew and grew, to add personality development or life adjustment to the list of educational goals and accomplishments. Not only would the schools falsely claim that they prepared children for their adult occupations, but they would audaciously add that they prepared children for life. Educators became the prime contenders for forming individual identity, taking that responsibility away from the family, the traditional conferrer of identity on its offspring.

Each self-interested constituency evaluated the worth of compulsory schooling according to its own lights. While business executives applied business techniques and values, educators measured students' behavior and academic performance, and parents boasted of their children's accomplishments or bemoaned their failures. However, once large numbers of children were required by law to attend school and more schools and more professionals became involved in the process of education, the question of whether compulsory schooling was desirable, necessary, or feasible, faded away. While nearly 2 million children, aged seven to thirteen, were still working in 1910 and not attending school, the overwhelming majority of children in that age bracket attended elementary school.

As late as 1920, however, high school was still not an accepted part of the compulsory schooling scenario. Children under fourteen, reluctantly or willingly, attended school at least part of the year; but only one-third of the fourteen- to seventeen-year-old school population went to high school.[11] Certainly this was not because schools did not try to recruit and entice young people to attend. The twentieth-century school establishment has kept expanding its goals and promises, though rarely delivering on them. As historian Henry Perkinson has said of the twentieth-century American school: "This sorting out of people according to their probable destinies was a totally new function for the American school. In the past the American school had not decided the probable destiny of the children who attended it."[12] The longer children went to school, the more promises were made to them, their parents, and taxpayers as to the wonders the school would perform. Advanced schooling, educators promised, would prepare students for life and for a more prestigious and profitable job. No small goals.

By the time of the Great Depression, compulsory elementary education had taken a firm hold. The sustained economic catastrophe of the 1930s gave high school education its needed impetus. The single largest group of unemployed workers were young adolescents and adults. Fully one-third of the 15 million unemployed in 1933 were in the fifteen- to twenty-four-year-old age group.[13] Joseph Kett has noted that "only during the depression did it become routine for boys to finish high school."[14] There was nothing else to do. The New Deal programs such as the Civilian Conservation Corps and the National Youth Administration provided jobs for a very small number of unmarried young men but they could not possibly absorb the large numbers of unemployed youth. Some observers estimated that there were 2–3 million youth just "hanging around."[15] Compulsory schooling took on another meaning. There were no other viable alternatives. Neither the private nor the public work place could employ the energetic youth so they reluctantly returned to school. Work had provided young adults with their sense of worth and accomplishment; work had absorbed much of their youthful energy. But in a no-work world, the only option was attending school.

To deal with this often obstreperous population who questioned its worth, educators introduced "reforms" into high school life. They created student government to give the students a sense of participation in decision making;

they created junior high schools to segregate the young adolescents from the teenagers; and they inadvertently created the conditions for a distinct youth culture. Extracurricular activities, for example, became fashionable in the late 1920s and continued in the 1930s as a new and essential part of the high school program. Educational journals discussed the varying kinds of extracurricular activities and evaluated their worth. One professional administrator of such a program wrote in 1932, "With more and more emphasis on shorter working hours, the five-work-day week, the machine-made article which is replacing the hand-made one, etc., it becomes necessary to provide for unoccupied time, for a worthy use of leisure. The place to begin training for this is in school, since the school is replacing the home."[16]

By reaching out into the larger culture and identifying social changes there, the educators justified a change within the school as an appropriate response. Needless to say, a whole new subspecialty arose as a result with an expanded professional staff; during the hard-pressed 1930s, however, classroom teachers had to double as coaches and advisers of extracurricular activities. More pertinent perhaps is that school expanded its hold over students, supervising their after-school hours and shaping their leisure-time activities. In this way, school became the arbiter of more and more parts of the student's life. The imperialistic impulse is clearly evident.

Each reform was heralded as the solution to the "youth problem." Indeed, one can link the identifying of the youth problem with the increased enrollment of adolescents in high schools, where, suddenly, large numbers of youths were clustered together. The study of adolescence became a flourishing industry as school enrollment increased; psychologists, parent-teacher councils, and social commentators discussed the difficulties of youth in countless conferences and publications, perhaps as an attempt to explain the creation of new activities or programs. Educators, faced with a large, new, unpredictable, and older student population, had to invent new ways of dealing with them. To make their actions understandable and respectable, educators often discussed them in terms of noble concepts such as "teaching American democracy" and "preparing students for life." With a mixture of intention and accident, schools increased in size and influence; in so doing, they had to explain, to themselves and to the taxpayers, what they were doing. Beginning with culturally accepted reasons (we are creating good citizens, preparing youth for the adult world) they expanded their goals (life adjustment, personality development), inventing new courses of study, new specialties, and new reasons for their own further expansion.

As human expectations change, so do human perceptions of self. If I as a student am expected to learn about myself and define myself in school, I will work toward that goal or feel that I am a failure. If I am expected to declare a major subject area of interest, I am defining myself in one way; failure to perform successfully within that area will result in a loss of self-esteem as well as genuine fear for the future.

Similarly, to avoid student failure, and to recognize the diversity of student needs and interests, schools expanded their course offerings and activities. They began to take on the structure and the character of a cafeteria. They increasingly gave the students, their parents, and the public-at-large the impression that multiple paths for success were available; if one failed, another was possible. No decisions were irrevocable, no course of study sacrosanct.

By the end of World War II, the elementary and high schools of America claimed the attendance of the majority of the youth group. Slightly over 50 percent of the seventeen-year-olds graduated from high school in 1940 in dramatic contrast to only 6.4 percent in 1900.[17]

The comprehensive high school, the eclectic compromise of varying American interest groups, claimed to provide basic, vocational, and intellectual courses for all students, but high school education was often gender segregated. In keeping with the overall culture's view that the adult destiny of daughters was predetermined, young girls were counseled into home economics and sewing courses; if they might have to work as adult women, they were advised to take the female vocational course track and study shorthand and typing. Bright, middle- and upper-class girls were permitted liberal arts programs, so they could be lively companions to their professional husbands.

By the 1950s, a vibrant youth culture was already evident in high schools. American teenagers looked alike, ate the same food, danced to the same music, adored the same pop-culture heroes, and used the same vernacular. Thanks to compulsory schooling, they had a uniform place to go during their adolescent and early adult years; thanks to compulsory schooling, they shared the same dreams and hopes; and thanks to compulsory schooling, they received the same fallible education. Segregated in place and legislated for a definite time to schooling, American youths responded by creating a subculture that had elements of the adult culture as well as values of its own.

Since the 1950s, public schooling has become an enormously expensive enterprise, capturing more and more of the taxpayers' money. Whether the satisfaction rate matches the cost is doubtful. However, compulsory elementary and high school has become accepted. While the young workers interviewed by Helen Todd in 1913 preferred work to school, the youth growing up in the post–World War II period knew of no alternative. Compulsory schooling appeared as the accepted and exclusive option. When sociologist Patricia Cayo Sexton asked sixth graders in East Harlem in the 1960s what they thought of school, they said:

You go to school to get an education so when you grow up you can get a decent job, and you can have a high school diploma. You can go to a decent junior high, and then you can go to a decent high, and go to a decent college, and get a decent job. When we grow up it'll be the nuclear age, and we couldn't do the jobs our fathers do. They'll be done by machines.

If you don't go to school you'll be a nobody. You'll be a drifter all your life.

School's OK, cause when you get a job you got to count things in your mind, not on your fingers. If you don't go to school you grow up to be dumb. You won't be able to get a job.

Whenever I wake up I say, you better study, you know, to get a better education. If you study now, you could become something big. When you grow up you get a good job.[18]

Schooling had become synonymous with a better future. Professional educators, politicians, business executives, and parents convinced themselves—and everyone else—that an inadvertent necessity had become desirable and essential.

By midcentury, compulsory schooling had become an accepted feature of twentieth-century life. All children were expected to attend high school. People no longer debated the issues. The age of compulsory schooling had increased steadily throughout the century so that all children and youth to the age of sixteen were required to attend school. What was once a fluid situation in which other alternatives were available for young people had become a closed, no-alternative situation. As compulsory schooling increased, apprenticeship programs decreased. The few apprenticeship programs that remained were carefully controlled by labor unions and often required a high school diploma of its applicants.

The sixth graders in East Harlem accurately reflected the contemporary popular view that not only does school prepare an individual for adult work but it also is the conferrer of identity, of meaning, and of purpose in life. "If you don't go to school you'll be a nobody" is a poignant and succinct statement of that view. The nineteenth-century school strove to inculcate moral principles to its students and left job training to the family, the apprentice system, and the marketplace. It did not even conceive of its role as including identity formation. Students learned who they were with the help of the family and the community. The twentieth-century school has assumed two mammoth new goals—job training and identity formation—and most evidence suggests that they are not fulfilling either goal satisfactorily. A nineteenth-century farmer's son attended school to learn to read, write, and count; a twentieth-century city child is expected to learn these basic skills in addition to preparing for a vocation and developing a well-defined personality. These inflated purposes have promised an expansion of human possibilities while, in reality, they have restricted them. Educators, possibly more than any other group, have been responsible for defining people *only* in terms of their future occupation or profession. "You are what you are trained to earn a living at" has become the late twentieth-century's definition of self, a very limiting definition, propagated and perpetuated by educators desperate to justify themselves.

Educators are no more evil than any other group of individuals. Neither are they more susceptible to conspiracies. Rather, there appears to be an inevitable frame of reference that governs each self-interest group. In the case of educators, they recognized the expansion of years in school as an opportunity to be explored and exploited for their benefit. Their roles, their functions, their resources, and their rewards could be expanded in proportion, or possibly in greater proportion, to the increased size of the student body. Just as bureaucracy has inherent principles that govern its behavior despite the good intentions of reformer-administrators, so educator-administrators can always develop a rationale to justify their new program, their additional staff, and their need for more funds. The coup de grace, of course, the supreme example of collective self-aggrandizement of the educational establishment, was the joining of the concepts of education and identity; by convincing Americans that who you are can be determined and acquired in school, educators insured their future.

Personality development, at best a vague concept, is usually translated into social adjustment; emphasis is placed upon conformity, not creativity, upon passive acceptance, not critical detachment. Ironically, school, despite the educators, *has* become the place where self-definition is worked out, but only because school is where all the kids are. The learning, debating, and living occurs in the study halls, the corridors, the playground, and the lounges. The off-campus coffee shop, rather than the school library, is probably the setting for the most sustained consideration of how one should spend a day, what should be a person's values, how to resolve human conflicts, and how to plan for the future.

The schools have participated in creating the new American personality type: the cafeteria American. Students are encouraged to take courses in a variety of fields and to be conversant in many different areas. The school cafeteria offers a multitude of foods, catering to a wide range of tastes. The school athletic program and the academic program give students many alternatives; specialization is deferred until the post–high school educational experience, indeed to the graduate school level. Survey courses, rather than intense, narrowly focused courses, are the major substance of the high school and undergraduate curriculum. To know a little about a lot, rather than a lot about a little, is the American educational way. This commitment to breadth rather than depth and to variety rather than a single specialty encourages a superficial experimenting with different offerings but little discipline in mastery of a difficult subject matter. Students take an overview course in western civilization but never read Voltaire; others study general science without performing a laboratory experiment.

While practicing an eclecticism that teaches students that life is an infinite cafeteria to be sampled, professional educators try to emphasize the link between education and future job possibilities, and by inference, future adult identity, claiming that education will prepare students for the adult world. The meager skills taught in the schools neither prepare students for jobs nor for adult life's possibilities. It is only in this century that the school/work link has been cemented and self-identity has been reduced to one's work, which one supposedly learns in school. The identity-forming process, according to the educational establishment, can be accomplished solely in the schools. The family, work, peer group, cultural experiences, and simple life experiences no longer provide the rich complex that creates self-definition, or so imply educators. While job training and schooling became associated in the public mind in the pre–World War I period, schooling and identity formation became the new equation of the post–World War II period. Youths would discover themselves as well as their future occupation in school.

The ambitious claims and goals of the educational establishment, it seems to me, must be reexamined and scaled down. While choice in curricular offerings, athletic programs, and extracurricular activities is an inherently acceptable, if not desirable, feature of American education, it has been carried too far. By definition, professional educators should have some clear ideas about what constitutes a worthy education. Though no two educators may agree on everything, there is surely a significant core of essential courses that all students should take. Indeed, while the 1960s witnessed the vast expansion of the school-as-cafeteria, the 1980s have seen the reduction of the cafeteria's offerings.

But another more significant step remains: the recognition that the school is only one of the culture's agencies of value, only one of the sources of knowledge for all Americans. America's schools must reevaluate their purposes, with both high schools and colleges reducing their aims. Neither is the primary conferrer of identity, nor should it be.

Neither trains people adequately for their adult jobs. On-the-job training, even in the late 1980s, remains the primary place where doctors, lawyers, bank clerks, teachers, secretaries, and factory workers learn the ingredients of their jobs. Further, adult identity is based upon a richer and wider variety of values, interests, and talents than those gained from work. After all, other parts of the American cafeteria contribute as well.

In the 1980s, there are at least three surprising results of compulsory schooling: (1) the role reversal process by which adults imitate youth in dress and behavior; (2) the paradoxical consequence of an increase in youthful dependency; and (3) rather than school acting as a temporary way station on the way to real life, the school style and environment have become a substitute life, a life that is lived for more and more years by more and more people. People over thirty dress like teenagers, dance their dances, and drink their drinks. The play mentality characteristic of adolescents has become the accepted adult mentality, and adults have become arrested in the adolescent phase of development. Adults follow youths' lead in behavior, moral standards, and fashions, surely an unpredicted result of advocates of compulsory schooling. Adults are imitating youth, who by virtue of their elongated schooling, are more dependent, powerless, and irresponsible than ever before. Because of their prolonged period of dependency, youth seek immediate gratification in all of their activities and show little concern or interest in a society that has not given them decision-making power or the ability to earn a constructive livelihood. Without a vested interest in society, immediate pleasure is the only apparent alternative.

School's seductive qualities make it continually attractive so that more and more students choose to stay longer. Beginning in the 1960s, the public junior college and university started to take on the same characteristics as the high school. Compulsory schooling, though not mandated by law, included college in the 1970s. About 11 million people attended college in 1979, and the evidence suggests that the over twenty-five-year-old student is an increasing proportion of the student body. Schooling is becoming the life experience of a growing number of people for a large part of their lives. The school day and the school term is designed for the carefree and the unencumbered person. There is ample time to talk to friends, to drink coffee, to complain about assignments, and to play ball. One can dress as one likes, attend class if one wishes, and get by easily. It is respectable to go to school as opposed to hanging around a lamppost on a street corner or playing ball in the street. While school libraries are rarely overcrowded with zealous users, school cafeterias and lounges do a flourishing business.

The school life-style is a very appealing one. Educators, dependent upon students for their existence, encourage all forms of recruitment to insure the presence of large numbers of students on their campus. The youth culture, sometimes displaying a frivolous, impetuous character as well as plain silly features, should surprise no one since it is created by partly formed personalities in a very vulnerable and growing stage of life. Further, the very adults who criticize the youth culture hurry to profit from it. The marketers of America have courted youths and viewed them as a market for more and more products. The youth culture harmonizes with the larger American culture in that it upholds many of the same values: beauty, athletic prowess, and accomplishment in various areas. The major difference is the adolescent character that surrounds and shapes it. Stranded, without integral ties to a tradition, the youth culture has no past, no sacred texts, and no experience to determine the worth of its rules. They become the cafeteria Americans, the first generation of pickers and choosers, of quick accepters and rapid rejecters.

The overwhelming dominance of compulsory schooling

of the post–World War II period may distort our perspective on the subject of children and learning. It might not be untoward to suggest that the classroom experience for long periods of time is an aberrant experience placed between two distinctly different periods: the long expanse of time prior to the twentieth century when learning occurred by imitating one's elders and by apprenticing oneself to an experienced worker (practices still utilized in most of the world today), and the post–1980 world where sophisticated video communications with home computer terminals will revolutionize the subject of learning. Lifelong learning, in a variety of settings, is already replacing the age-segregated traditional classroom. Growing up in America in the twenty-first century may well include a wholly new series of educational experiences barely known to educators of the 1980s.

Not only is it very conceivable that the majority of human learning will occur in nontraditional settings in the future, but it is also paradoxically conceivable that the formal educational enterprise will remain alive, simply because it is such an immovable behemoth. Is it possible to visualize transferring vast numbers of high school and college teachers to America's factories, offices, and sundry other commercial establishments in which to conduct the required teaching? Or converting schools into profit-making enterprises? Not likely.

The industrial factory followed by the commercial, professional, and service industries established the compelling model for this century; children went to school to train for the new skills required by the new businesses and spent their wages on the ever-growing products, services, and entertainments coming out of those industries. Quantity and variety became the watchwords of twentieth-century industrialism and all of the allied activities it spawned. Variety, particularly, provided the framework, the value system, the people, and the methodology for the new consumerism; it became the basis for, the creator, and the perpetuator of the cafeteria approach to modern living. And it was in school that students were trained to participate in the new industrial order and to benefit from its fruits.

But the public school establishment, enriched and expanded by America's industrialism, became a self-perpetuating entity. It borrowed ideas, values, and programs from its sponsor, but it developed its own ideas. It also shared in the general cultural commitment to growth, variety, freedom of choice, and individual difference. It created, then, its own cafeteria within the larger cafeteria of America. It offered its students a bewildering variety of courses and programs that promised them knowledge, a sense of self-worth, and assurances of future happiness and success. Because the work world had fewer and fewer jobs for the growing numbers of young people (especially in the 1960s and 1970s), it encouraged longer and longer years of preparation for the students.

At the same time, teenagers were engaging in part-time work while attending high school. In 1980, 63 percent of the nation's high school seniors reported that they worked during the school year.[19] Two years later, the figure was 70 percent. The jobs held by the students were largely in service industries: as cashiers at fast-food restaurants or as clerks in department stores. They were not jobs that helped students prepare for their eventual occupation. While some experts praised student work as character building, most teachers and psychologists questioned its worth. Students had less time for their studies and for after-school activities. Further, they used, what one social psychologist called their "premature affluence" to buy the latest in video equipment, fashionable clothes, and expensive vacations.[20]

We have come full circle. While reporter Helen Todd wrote on children early in the century who liked to work because it gave them a sense of independence and accomplishment, 1980s students work part-time for many of the same reasons; the nickolodeon has been replaced by the video recorder.

Today, students become full-fledged participants in the consumer world. As teenagers, they have become experienced members of the cafeteria society. Because their tastes change rapidly, so do the objects of their purchases. In school, they may take consumer-education courses (a good example of the school imitating the marketplace), and in the marketplace, they may learn how expensive items can only be purchased by well-certified (that is, educated) people. And so they return to the classroom to gain more of what the marketplace offers.

Though I lament the endless buying that results from this process, I am more concerned with the mindless view that education's primary worth is its dollar return and its purchasing-power potential. Intelligent consumers can only be created when the educational process, rather than catering to the market, stands for a set of intellectual values separate from vocational and financial considerations.

I would advocate a very simple return to both basic and classical educational principles. Remove job training from the high schools and colleges; replace them with a rich assortment of humanities, social science, and natural science courses; offer students the opportunity to contemplate abstract and real questions that will not be posed by their employers but are essential to human development. Offer students the opportunity to become educated, to make intelligent, conscious choices; then not only the cafeteria of America can be enjoyed, based upon an informed and sensitive awareness of the possibilities offered, but life's riches outside the cafeteria can also be contemplated. True education allows students to understand the advantages and disadvantages of each set of options while recognizing that paths taken also result in rejected paths and important consequences. Then the benefits of compulsory schooling will become apparent, useful, and fulfilling.

Chapter

4

Children:
Before and After
the Rise of
the Youth
Culture

Some scholars credit or blame psychologist G. Stanley Hall with inventing adolescence. He identified, in his 1903 book *Adolescence,* a new stage in life, a period between childhood and adulthood. This period had its own special features, problems, and possibilities. But it was a clearly demarcated, separate time in human development. Doctors, teachers, parents, and preachers all had to recognize its existence, pay heed to its meaning, and adjust their actions and behaviors accordingly. The adolescent's physiological, psychological, and social makeup was different than that of a child's and an adult's. On this insight a whole new field of inquiry was built.

Appearing simultaneously with the increase of compulsory schooling (at least at the elementary school level), the professional students of adolescence merged with professional educators to segregate teenagers from younger children, to organize special workshops to consider their particular problems, and to counsel parents on the patience required to deal with this difficult constituency. Juvenile delinquency received more attention as did parent-teacher meetings. In the 1920s and 1930s, these themes and trends began to take hold, though they did not receive great support and popularity until after 1960 when the baby-boom population of the postwar period reached its adolescent years—the true flowering of the youth culture in all of its multifaceted dimensions.

Philosopher Hannah Arendt noted the rise of an autonomous youth culture in the 1950s and warned her readers that this boded ill for future generations: "Therefore by being emancipated from the authority of the adults the child has not been freed but has been subjected to a much more terrifying and truly tyrannical authority, the tyranny of the majority."[1] By segregating children from grown-ups, she argued, they had been banished from the adult world, and by implication, the adult world had served notice that they were not responsible for them; a nonconforming child had nowhere to go. "They are either thrown back upon themselves or handed over to the tyranny of their own group against which, because of its numerical superiority, they cannot rebel, with which, because they are children, they cannot reason, and out of which they cannot flee to any other world because the world of adults is barred to them."[2] Their choice, Arendt declared, was either conform to the youth groups' wishes, to become juvenile delinquents, or both.

By cutting children off from adults, as well as from children of other ages, adults forced children to create a group, an identifiable unity among themselves. According to Arendt, adults should assume vigorous responsibility for the temporary education of youth; young people should not become an autonomous, self-defined, power group. It is the responsibility of adults, she claimed, to prepare youth for the adult world, for assuming the tasks of adulthood. Thus, school during the youthful years, should only be a temporary way station on the road to adulthood.

Arendt believed that parents gave up authority over their children, thus giving rise to an autonomous youth culture. In my analysis, generational conflicts, first evident among the middle class and the new immigrants, resulted from the new industrialism; then schooling deepened and accentuated those same tensions. Arendt's analysis, though prescient in its anticipation of a youth culture, did not explain why parents abandoned their children. I would suggest a push-pull thesis: the push away from the old to benefit from the new opportunities combined with the pull of the group culture's promise of freedom, of excitement, and of autonomy.

Historically, the glimmering of an identifiable youth culture was first evident in the 1920s, a decade that saw a 20 percent rise in the size of the fourteen- to twenty-four-year-old population. It was most notable in the increasing numbers of college students, though college remained an elite experience until the 1960s. Manufacturers and sellers of clothing, cosmetics, and cigarettes all exploited the new college market of the 1920s and foreshadowed a trend that was only to expand enormously later in the century.

Indeed, a street culture, consisting of children of immigrants was already evident early in the century. Historian David Nasaw's recent historical study of city children noted that they were both workers and consumers of goods readily available on city streets.[3] Children sold newspapers, chewing gum, and sundry other things. They also observed the myriad of merchandise available for sale. "There were amusements, entertainments, and fashions to fit every pocketbook, different variations of the same basic model for different classes of urban customers."[4] The stage was then set: children became prime participants as both workers and buyers of America's growing stock of goods and pleasures.

Viviana A. Zelizer's recent study, *Pricing the Priceless Child,* suggests that during the fifty-year period from 1870 to 1930 America went from viewing children as economic units who could profit the family to sacred, economically useless creatures who were to be valued for themselves.[5] This framework harmonizes with my view that as American living became concentrated in cities, with children in school for longer and longer periods, and with improved communications, children became the focus of attention of all the different agencies of the culture. They assumed, however, a new economic function: as consumers of the ever increasing products of American manufacturing. Children went from being economic producers to economic consumers. Moreover, as objects of concern, they became products themselves, studied by various professionals; parents began investing in them as well, and a host of institutions, profit-making organizations, and schools benefited from the new attention given to children.

Prior to the 1960s, youth was still a temporary stage of life, one accepted as such by both adults and children alike. Though children were essentially trained to engage in the pleasures of the marketplace, they were also expected to become producers and workers as adult members of society. Since the 1960s, the trends developed earlier became more widespread. America's industrial capacity moved beyond fulfilling basic needs and produced surplus goods that had to be sold. Further, growing numbers of youths became the natural market for more goods and services. The size of the fourteen- to twenty-four-year-old population had risen steadily since 1950 with a 10 percent rise from 1950 to 1960, a spectacular 52 percent rise from 1960 to 1970, and an 11 percent rise from 1970 to 1980.[6] The increased number in this age group, of course, make their every action and gesture noticeable and significant. While immigrant children were exposed to modest imitations of fads and fashions of the middle and upper classes, the new youth market, more middle class and affluent than ever before, became the target for luxury goods as well.

More importantly, marketers catered to their faddishness and their interest in the silly and the flimsy. Business accepted the youthful stage as one existing indefinitely, and, ever watchful for new markets for their products, immediately discerned the value of the youth market and began gearing their sales campaigns to them. The commercial sellers upheld the stereotypical image of youth and then confirmed it by exploiting it. One business executive in the early 1970s counseled: "The manufacturer of a fad product must be ready to move quickly into something else."[7]

While manufacturers geared up for quick product changes and bombarded the markets with more and more things, sociologists lamented the faddishness of youth, as if that trait were unique to that age group. Youth shared the same essential American values with their parents. They admired athletic prowess and natural beauty; they believed in competition, in accomplishment, and in victory. American youths' ready responsiveness to the "buy, buy" mentality was another shared value. They were imitating adult behavior, not establishing new patterns of action.

The interaction between the producers of goods and services and the expanding youth market resulted in a bewildering, ever changing, flexible definition of youths' values and tastes. Marketers were anxious to identify the needs and dreams of their new market, while youth, in the very process of self-definition, eagerly sought any guidance they could get in working out their identities. Youth declared their likes and dislikes, gut reactions to goods, and fashionable ideologies only to have the marketers produce goods that reflected these values. The manufacturer's commitment was to produce salable goods, an amoral devotion to the profit motive.

If the flower children of the 1960s wanted to return to nature, the business people of America accommodated them with a large line of natural foods, leathercrafts, bicycles, and camping equipment. Socially conscious youth of the late 1960s found manufacturers happy to make T-shirts, buttons, and bumper stickers that advertised their particular cause. Because youths did not have a firm idea of who they were, their wishes often changed; fads and fashions substituted for deeply felt values. Since industry begins with the assumption that once they can identify a market and its needs (or create needs), they can proceed to sell to that market, they changed their products and services as youth changed its fads.

Indeed, there was a dizzying proliferation of fad products in the 1950s and 1960s, unknown prior to the surplus capitalism phase and the growth of the youth population and subculture. Wham-O Manufacturing Company of San Gabriel, California, the manufacturer of the hula hoop, sold $45 million worth of hula hoops in five months of 1958, an all-time record for the period, but had to invent other fads such as the frisbee to keep up with competitors for the consumers' market of new and newer fads. Some fads lasted months, others years. The 1955 Davy Crockett craze lasted only eight months but spawned over 500 items at a cost to parents of $100 million.[8] T-shirts and sweatshirts became popular in the early 1960s and continue to be a successful item, though the subjects and slogans of the shirts change with the changing times.

Social commentators tried to classify fads and explain the explosion of buyable popular cultural items. Gloria Steinem contributed "Return-Trip Pop" and "Classic Pop" as two recognizable categories for the bewildering variety of fads, fashions, and phenomena of youth. Humphrey Bogart movies, football, Jean Harlow, and Monopoly exemplified the former category while the Marx Brothers comedies, Elizabeth Taylor, and *Catcher in the Rye* qualified as Classic Pop.[9] There was no serious attempt to explain the reasons for the item's popularity. Everyone was encouraged to make his own lists, another faddish expression of the late 1970s.

One observer quoted in a *Newsweek* summary of youth's fads worried " . . . that the "youth cult" may be leading the real youths to wrong conclusions about how they should act as adults. Teenagers of today . . . may grow up to imitate tomorrow's teenagers . . . thereby setting up a cycle of permanent adolescence."[10]

Newsweek, a frequent surveyor of fads, ended the discussion on a sanguine note assuring its readers that youth's fancies were temporary and no one need worry about them. Business discussions, on the other hand, took an amoral attitude toward it all and concerned itself with ways to capitalize on the growing affluence of the youth market. A *Business Week* article discussed the new market and the new market research techniques it required. Business executives were advised to take advantage of the fads, to recognize the speed with which they grew and declined, and to be adaptable to the changing tastes of youth.[11] A commitment to quick change of product to remain relevant and profitable characterized both business and human behavior. The old American virtues of adaptability and inventiveness became the basis for the cafeteria mentality of the 1980s.

In recent years, decision makers have continually expanded their definition of the youth market. While the fourteen- to twenty-four-year-old boundary used to define youth, there are current discussions of youth that define the age group as twelve to thirty-two.[12] One could even lower the age to nine or ten and expand it to forty. This trend demonstrates the imperialistic tendency of the fad producers to extend the youthful stage to a lifetime. Prior to the twentieth century, children and youth played baseball together, wrestled together, and played tag together. Girls of eight and thirteen played with dolls and joined in a game of dominoes. With school instituting age-segregated classes, play activities have also been segregated according to age. Further, as younger and younger children have allowances (and nagging voices), they have become consumers as well, a fact well known to the marketers. Comic book producers, for example, know that there are 40 million potential buyers of their product. They also delight in the fact that over 80 percent of the seven- to eleven-year-olds read comic books, resulting in a $200 million industry.[13]

Researchers Brian Sutton-Smith and B. G. Rosenberg compared three historical studies of children's game preferences done in the years 1891, 1921, and 1959. One striking conclusion was that certain games remained favorites over the 68-year period. Baseball, football, swimming, and dolls, for example, appeared on all of the lists as favorite games. Though the traditional "girls games" and "boys games" remained, the girls began playing more of the boys games as time went on. Dolls ranked first for girls in 1891 and eighth in 1921 and 1959. Boys narrowed their preferences to fewer sports in 1959 than they had done in the 1890s.[14] But the most interesting conclusion that emerged from this study was that, as of 1959, most of the children's games were simple, easy to play, easy to organize, and inexpensive. Tag and hide-and-seek, for example, remained favorites of both sexes in all periods studied.

In the 1960s, children's games took a commercial turn. They became more organized, formal, and expensive. Boys were organized into Little League games rather than simple spontaneous baseball games. Athletics became a serious and professionally managed enterprise, even for children. Expensive board games became popular thanks to heavy television advertising. Elaborate dolls and models of favorite TV characters sold at toy counters; cowboys, spacemen, baseball players, and rock stars became doll-like characters for the amusement of both sexes, but more importantly for the enrichment of the entrepreneurs. Capitalizing on the heavy television viewing of young children, advertisers hawked their toys before their naive viewers. Another youth market had been identified and categorized. The manufacturers of children's games have become another force intent upon segregating youth, in this case young children, into a separate subculture or market. One business executive advised his colleagues that they should appeal to young children because "now is the time to build loyalty."[15]

Grace and Fred Hechinger noted the emergence of a distinct youth market in a 1965 *Esquire* article entitled "In the Time It Takes You to Read These Lines the American Teenagers Will Have Spent $2378.22."[16] In an essay replete with examples of how teenagers have become a major consuming group in America, the Hechingers concluded: "Adolescents, naturally insecure, find life rudderless in a world which relies excessively on their judgments and selections."[17] Teenagers may have purchased 9 percent of all new cars in the mid-1960s as well as many other consumer items, but they were unsure of themselves and of the direction in which they were going. The "rudderlessness" of American youth made them apt targets for the cafeteria approach to life. They became the first experimenters with the "pick, choose, and discard" mentality.

While the teenage market accounted for half the movie-going audience in 1965, a 1978 estimate of the twelve- to thirty-two-year-old market reported that they represented 80 percent of the movie-going audience.[18] The growth in the youth population as well as the greater number of years designated as youthful years has resulted in a huge market, a market that voraciously consumes rock records, cameras, cosmetics, and cars in greater and greater amounts. The sales of rock records, for example, has grown spectacularly, thanks to the youth market; while the rock record business reached sales of $2.4 billion in 1976, the following year, sales topped $4 billion.[19] It has only been the video and audio cassette explosion of the 1980s that has caused the decline in record sales.

Prior to the baby boom generation (1946–1964), adults looked to other adults for understanding and controlling children. Preachers, teachers, and doctors explained to everyone what children were like as well as what they should be like. Further, when children appeared in the popular media, such as child movie stars, they were admired by parents even more than by children. Child stars portrayed adult images and values of what children should be. Two very popular child stars of the 1930s and 1940s, Shirley Temple, a real little girl, and Baby Snooks, an adult Fanny Brice imitating a child on the radio, epitomize this point. Both represented American adulthood's idea of amusing children; they were both coached and directed by adults. Shirley Temple was turned into a living commodity as well; her picture appeared on coloring books and picture postcards, on theater marquees, and in store windows. Between 1935 and 1938, she was the top box office star in America. Newspaper pictures of audiences going into a Shirley Temple movie reveal a preponderance of adults (male adults) who attended her movies. She became America's symbol of childhood. The Temple ideal was precisely that, an ideal, not a realistic characterization of children. Before children and youths became a formidable force in their own right, they were fantasy projections of adults.

Popular child stars such as Shirley Temple embodied American ideals about children; they did not necessarily document the lives of children. Audiences also projected adult hopes and wishes onto their child stars. The Shirley Temple image was one half of the archetypal dualism that Western society has held about children since the Enlightenment. Temple was the good, cute, perky child, while Baby Snooks was the Puritan view of children, naturally evil and in need of taming. This dualism with shadings in between still represent most of the essential portraits of children in popular culture. From Shirley Temple to Gary Coleman, Americans love their media children to be cute and clever, rarely a nuisance, and always good company.

Shirley Temple was admired by children and adults alike because she stood for accepted American values; she was cute but not overwhelmingly beautiful. She could be the little girl next door. Shirley Temple was both of her times and better than her times. She uplifted sorrowful spirits during the height of the Great Depression; she helped confused adults find their way while retaining her childlike posture. In *Little Miss Marker* (1934), for example, she helped gamblers resolve their differences and got hard-hearted adults to soften up. Seemingly, a child's simplicity and directness could deal successfully with adults' problems. In many of her movies, Shirley Temple played the part of an orphan; but rather than being vulnerable, befitting an orphan's life, she became the independent force, capable of solving others' conflicts. At age six, she received a special Academy Award honoring her accomplishments. "The award is bestowed because Shirley Temple brought more happiness to millions of children and millions of grown-ups than any child of her years in the history of the world."[20]

In *The Little Colonel* (1935), Temple reconciled her mother with her recalcitrant grandfather. The little girl with the lovely curls and the winning smile was the peacemaker, the harmonizer needed by depression audiences. To say that a seven-year-old had the capacity to solve problems beyond the ken of adults stretched credulity, but it surely pleased her fans. In *Heidi* (1937), she convinced her infidel grandfather to attend church; she also became a matchmaker and taught a crippled girl to walk. "Dear God," she prayed at the end of the film, "please make every little boy and girl in the world just as happy as I am."[21]

In most Shirley Temple movies, the major interaction was between Temple and a male figure, her father or a surrogate father. Through her actions, she not only asserted the importance of children but forced adults to behave morally so that they would not corrupt children. She had adventures endearing her to the children in the audience who, like their parents, went to the movies to experience excitement vicariously. She represented goodness and un-complicated solutions to human problems. She was direct, active, and unwilling to take no for an answer. Temple's character was a heroine who possessed all of the qualities Americans invested in their adult heroines as well. She was the projection of children at their best, their most pristine, sweet, and natural state.

Baby Snooks, the creation of adult star Fanny Brice, represented the darker view of children. Snooks, in contrast to sweet and lovely Shirley Temple, was mischievous, ornery, and always in trouble with her father. Again, however, the father-daughter relationship was the essential one. Snooks always aggravated her father. In one episode, Daddy rehearsed Snooks to tell the movie cashier that she was a child; she loudly replied: "Is five too much?"

"This picture better be good," retorted her father.

Snooks answered, "It is."

"How do you know?" her father asked.

"I've seen it twice," responded Snooks.

Throughout the movie, she talked and the sequence ended with her father hitting her, not an uncommon ending of a Baby Snooks show. When she was asked to testify at a trial where her father was the defendant, he counseled her, "Tell the Judge in your own words, Snooks."

She replied, "Didn't you want me to tell it in your words, Daddy?"

While Shirley Temple resolved crises to everyone's satisfaction, Snooks created confusion, consternation, and frustration for all around her. She insulted her father's boss at the dinner table, outwitted her father at a test of intelligence, and fooled everyone on Halloween. Most Baby Snooks radio shows ended with Snooks crying after her father hit her for her latest escapade. The stark contrast between Shirley Temple and Baby Snooks offered audiences two very different, though both very popular, views of children. The wisecracking Snooks is every parent's nightmare and angelic Shirley is every parent's dream. Each is an exaggeration, a more extreme version of possible reality, but both are adult contrivances. Adults determined the outcome.

The Hollywood image makers of the 1930s assumed that they understood the wishes of an audience consisting of children and adults. All ages and both sexes went to the same movies, in stark contrast to today. Further, there were no extensive opinion polls taken of audience taste as there was the unspoken, and apparently accurate, assumption that the producers and writers at Twentieth Century Fox understood the needs of the public. The growth of the movie market, in all of its diversity, surely resembled the growing cafeteria of America, but at that state, it was still being directed by the adults, not the children.

With the expansion of the youth population coupled with the breakdown in adult authority, commercial sellers of pop stars and products took their cues from their youthful audiences. The 1940s witnessed the beginning of an identifiable culture when bobby soxers, a new term invented to describe a new reality, flocked to the concerts of the first certified pop hero, Frank Sinatra. Newspapers, records, and radios announced his appearances, played his songs, and gauged audience interest. The economy had improved after the Great Depression, and bobby soxers could afford to pay seventy-five cents for a ticket to a Frank Sinatra concert and the requisite dollars for his records. Intense and concentrated promotion of a Sinatra concert was sure to attract loyal fans. Once the loyalty of the masses was assured, free publicity replaced managed public relations methods. In fact, the fans became news stories themselves.

Frank Sinatra in the 1940s, Elvis Presley in the 1950s, and the Beatles in the 1960s captured the hearts and imaginations of American youth. Though it is difficult if not impossible to define the essential reason for their incredible success, it is possible to describe their similarities. First, Sinatra, Elvis, and the Beatles all conveyed a youthful appearance, though none were in the age group to which they appealed. All identified with the young and spoke in terms of "we" in discussions with their audiences. Frank Sinatra was twenty-five years old, a husband and father, when he left the Tommy Dorsey band in September 1942 and began singing solo. To his fans, however, he was vulnerable and young. "I wear bow ties, sport jackets and sweaters, and kids like 'em!" Sinatra noted. "I'm their type."[22] His slim, 137-pound frame appealed to the bobby soxers as well.

Elvis was twenty-one-years-old when his bump and grind singing routine attracted national attention in 1956. "Girls describe Presley," according to one account, "as a combination of Marlon Brando and the late James Dean, and boys admire the exaggeration of his rhythmic rock 'n' roll." Boys also imitated his duck-tail haircut, black leather jacket, and walking style. He was the "baddest," one young girl said, and " . . . when I say the "baddest," that means the greatest."[23] Presley's style epitomized youthful rebellion, the "I don't give a damn" attitude adolescents often felt toward adult authority but could not express. Elvis expressed it with vigor, and on the Ed Sullivan Show, no less. He acted out youthful rebellion and got away with it. The Beatles were all over twenty years old when they first toured the United States in 1964, but they too appeared to identify with youth, not with the adult world. Their long hair, bangs, and personalized clothes styles symbolized their independence from the respectable social establishment.

All had their greatest appeal to young girls. Though older, married women went to the Riobamba night club in New York to see Sinatra perform, it was the bobby soxers who formed his most devoted following. One adult observer of a Sinatra concert said: "Four-fifths of those present are of the feminine sex and of those, at least four-fifths belong to the bobby-socks brigade, age perhaps twelve to sixteen."[24] According to Marjorie Diven, who was in charge of Sinatra's fan mail, his average fan was a fourteen-year-old girl living in a small town. By some estimates, there were 2000 Frank Sinatra fan clubs in America in 1944. Similarly, the Elvis fans were primarily young girls of the same impressionable age and disposition. Fourteen-year-old girls in Fort Worth were known to carve Elvis' name on their forearms with clasp knives, and they all swooned at his concert appearances. While Presley was at Fort Hood, Texas for army training in 1958, he received 15,000 letters a week. When the Beatles toured the United States, the police departments in the tour cities shivered with dismay and frustration. One spokesman for the Astor Theater where they appeared described the audience as: "They're 99 $^{44}/_{100}\%$ teenagers with a smattering of adults—the same bunch that went for Elvis."[25]

Though psychologists and social commentators labored to explain the reason for the colossal success of these pop culture heroes, no one emerged with a satisfactory explanation. Some psychologists noted the excessive, newly discovered sexual energy of adolescents, especially impressionable young girls, and intimated that this was the reason for the excessive histrionics; others noted the mass behavior that overtakes large crowds and allows normally prudent, self-contained individuals to behave in unpredictable (to themselves and to others) ways. Still others dismissed the teenagers' behavior as characteristic of irrational adolescence. Surely devoted fans of all these entertainers discovered that they held a rare power over their parents in the sound war. The louder they played Elvis' records, the more they irritated their parents and guaranteed the price of a ticket to a concert if only they lowered the volume. Mothers lamented their daughters' insistence that they would just die if they did not attend a Beatles concert, and faithful Sinatra fans sat through four shows at the Paramount without leaving their seats.

Besides the youthful appearance of these pop cultural heroes and their open flaunting of society, they all evoked an image of vulnerability, needing the support of their fans for comfort, security, and assurance. They mirrored the adolescent fear of rejection. They were validated by the approving squeals of their audience; they confirmed their worth, the worth of their unique music, and their audiences' worth in the intricate process of performing. Elvis, after all, was an outsider, a Southern boy singing black rhythms before white audiences, a rural boy singing for urban folk. Sinatra's voice was not as sweet nor his manner as firmly middle class as was swooner Bing Crosby's or Rudy Vallee's. He was a poor boy from New Jersey, a simple fellow just like you and me. The Beatles' Liverpool origins were widely publicized. They were English, working class, a far cry from the American middle-class audience who bought their records and attended their concerts. They were outsiders on a good will tour to the new continent and their fans proved undyingly hospitable.

Sinatra, Elvis, and the Beatles all took a popular musical form and added their unique interpretation to it. Sinatra sang traditional love ballads with his personalized delivery. He paid a great deal of attention to the lyrics of a song and when he looked at the women in the audience while singing "As Time Goes By," they dutifully screeched in approval. Ballads had traditionally been sung to older women; Sinatra gave the words emphasis and meaning for bobby soxers. With a curl of hair falling on his forehead and his bow tie perched at a jaunty angle, he sang each word with feeling. Elvis blended the black rhythm and blues beat with country music and gave white audiences an accelerated rhythm to dance and scream to. The fast pace, the physical gyrations of the accompanying dance, and the sheer loudness of the music blocked out the lyrics. "You Ain't Nothing But a Hound Dog" catapulted to the top of the charts in 1956 and stayed there for months. Some critics were puzzled by the spectacular success of the Beatles and complained that they were crude imitators of Elvis and early rock 'n' roll. Others credited them with building on the Elvis tradition and inventing more creative and sophisticated musical rhythms. The Beatles' lyrics covered many subjects and fans searched for their comments on LSD, free sexuality, and spontaneous living.

They all used personal appearance tours to promote their latest records or movies. Their records remained at the top of the charts for years. They all used the electronic media expertly. Fans knew the music of their idols before they went to a concert. The radio stations playing their records gave the heroes ample exposure. The concert became a happening, a separate and exciting experience that only deepened and enhanced their already proven devotion. Attending a concert was not an introduction to the star for most; it was a confirmation of their loyalty, a declaration of their faith and commitment. The more successful the star became, the more delighted the fan. Newspapers and magazines published innumerable articles describing how Sinatra, the son of a firefighter in Hoboken, New Jersey became a millionaire within a year after he became a solo singer. When Elvis achieved the inimitable position in his day of having sold 100 million records for RCA in ten years, his fans rejoiced. Beatles fans could watch the spectacular rise of their idols and note with awe and admiration that between the years 1962 and 1964, they earned between 10 and 20 million dollars.

Fans remained loyal to this trio of pop culture heroes for years, though new idols quickly came and went in an effort to achieve the same enduring fame. It was the stars in each of these cases who dropped out, slackened their pace, or changed their artistic direction. Sinatra lessened his personal appearances in favor of his radio shows and, later, for a movie career. Elvis stopped appearing in public from 1960 to 1969 and though his records continued to sell, his absence from the public arena lowered his visibility and popularity. The Beatles split up in 1971 and thus ended their immensely profitable collaboration. But in all cases, their records and movies continued to turn a profit for them. The new generation of twelve-year-olds found new idols in the Rolling Stones, Jefferson Airplane, and other rock groups, but none of the 1970s or 1980s groups equalled Sinatra, Elvis, or the Beatles in popularity and longevity.

Sinatra's personal delivery of a love song, Elvis' openly sexual rendering of a rock 'n' roll song, and the Beatles spoofing the establishment all appealed to the respective youth generation that made each of them popular. All shared a style of rebellion, flaunting majoritarian values. They sang of illicit love, the individual's needs and rights over all criticism, and the wish to be externally free, all subjects that appealed enormously to youth. Indeed, they catered to their audiences in the same way that comic book producers appealed to theirs. They had few prescriptions for adult happiness, but many suggestions about youthful vulnerability, strength, and spirit. In tribute to their heroes, youth bought a variety of items that were identified with their heroes, and in so doing, they became regular buyers of more and more goods.

American youths, sharers of many adult cultural values, have demonstrated an equal interest in consuming goods. Electronic musical equipment and instruments, rock concerts and rock albums, expensive leather boots, and a proliferation of denim in all clothing styles and all costs are only a few of their favorite products. Upon reflection, it seems that advanced capitalism, ever watchful for new buyers, would explore and exploit the growing numbers of young people. Not anticipated of course is how powerful the buying impulse has become; how it has become a value in and of itself. A further unexpected consequence has been the blurring of the "adult" world. While a rock concert is still primarily attended by youths, rock records are being purchased by a wider age group. Fifty-year-old men wore hairpieces, gold jewelry, and colorful shirts and danced the latest disco dances with twenty-year-old girls in the 1970s; suburban couples learned disco dancing in their communities and frequented the disco lounges with people ranging in age from eighteen to fifty-five.

Rather than four age groups in our society (childhood, youth, adulthood, and old age), there now appears to be emerging only three: childhood, youth, and old age. Even as the number of adolescents decreases in the late 1980s, their style, mentality, and outlook pervade society. Further, since youths of the 1960s, the largest number in generations, are now "adults," the "yuppie generation," they still retain their commitment to their youthful life-style, and in so doing, guarantee the merging of the two age groups. To breed buying habits, marketers attack younger and younger children. Whereas the 1960s advertisers believed in building brand loyalty among teenagers, today, six- and seven-year-olds are being trained to purchase, to identify brand names, and to encourage their parents to buy more and buy more often. In this way, the manufacturers insure their futures. Getting and spending worried the poet Wordsworth as England was just beginning to industrialize; imagine his terror if he observed current getting and spending patterns in America! As Alex Inkeles remarked in a recent essay, "The consumption ethic has replaced the Protestant ethic."[26]

In the past, youths abandoned their distinctive youthful manner, dress, and hairstyle when they entered the adult business world. As recently as the late 1960s, a long-haired, eighteen-year-old man cut his hair before applying for a job at a bank. Though a man with shoulder-length hair still is looked at with suspicion, all men began growing their hair longer in the early 1970s, and so the distinction between youthful rebellion as symbolized in longer hair became blurred with young bankers sporting a longer hairstyle, a mustache, and in some cases a well-trimmed beard. Youthful expressions became accepted in the business world as well, and the lines between the identifiable, temporary youth world and the adult world became even more blurred. Both teenagers and adult men cut their hair into shorter styles by the 1980s making the transition from adolescent to adult imperceptible.

The tendency of adults to imitate youthful styles, rather than the other way around, may lead to confusion on the part of youth. What can they do to establish their differences, their discontent, their temporary wish to rebel, if adults imitate them? The frantic search for newness may be an unconscious desire to change quickly so that they can avoid the slavish imitation of their elders. By constantly discovering new styles, new fads, and new heroes they can stay ahead of their imitators. Since youth viewed their fashions and tastes as temporary amusements and rebellions, they may be puzzled by the admiration their behavior evokes in their elders. Similarly, since they have no guides for their behavior, except their own impulsive nature, they must wonder why established adults, people who ostensibly operate within a well-defined code of behavior, follow them.

Indeed, one could argue that the whole process of growing up has taken a reverse direction; chronological adults choose not to grow up, not to change the behavior, attitudes, and styles they learned as adolescents. The generational conflict described in an earlier chapter disappears as parents follow the lead of their children. The distinct youth culture, once assigned to a particular age group, has become the youth-adult culture of 1980s America. From this perspective, the 1980s youthful search may not be a search at all. Rather, it may be a constant holding action or a continuous experiment with living in the present as a cafeteria personality. Benjamin, the antihero of the movie *The Graduate* (1967), a college graduate with not the foggiest idea of what he would do with the rest of his life, aptly symbolized the emerging cafeteria American of both sexes. He is the patchwork product of an experimental educational system, of selfish, insecure parents, and of a youth culture that loses interest in issues rapidly. His very indecisiveness and general aimlessness were viewed as assets by the youthful movie audience who identified with him. The painfully unfinished quality of Benjamin's personality seemed to capture the new American white, middle-class youth of twenty-one, the new generation of questing kids. While Benjamin neither lamented nor heralded his indecisiveness, his contemporaries made a virtue out of those traits. Not only were youths told not to trust anyone over thirty, but also anyone who was sure about anything.

Experimenting became a virtue in itself, change was inherently good, and life became an unending process of self-discovery. The mental health profession proliferated in the late 1960s as more and more people accepted this new message. Looking inward, abandoning consistency as a virtue, focusing upon personal pleasure, and suspending judgment of everything became the new value system of youth and adults by the late 1970s. The temporary value system of adolescents become the permanent value system of all adults. The new age reveled in its antihistorical and antitraditional view of life. The past was to be ignored, not even actively rejected. Reform groups such as the feminists also repudiated the past since, they reasoned, traditional models and explanations prescribed women's roles, an undesirable condition in an age that stressed individual liberation. The contemporary generation has turned American values onto its head; while decisiveness, individual determination, and hard work were prized values in the past, they are presently scorned or suspected. Politicians with strong profiles are eschewed while blurred images are preferred. Political and business heroes have been replaced with rock star heroes, performers whose most outrageous behavior is admired.

The cafeteria personality, created by the mass-production assembly line and the academic assembly line, is ubiquitous in modern America. The American love of novelty and newness, fostered by an affluent consuming citizenry, has compartmentalized personality, identity, goods, and values. Nothing is beyond the reach of the imperialistic cafeteria mentality. So Benjamin's lack of a coherent identity and his equal attention to everything and nothing, eerily but accurately reflect the new hero of the cafeteria mind. It was only a matter of time before the effects of compulsory schooling, a sophisticated industrial technology, and the American value system coincided to produce this fragmented, fad-ridden person.

In harmony with the cafeteriamania is a return to romantic values. Romanticism's emphasis upon individual process and self-discovery over goal-directed behavior fits neatly into the new mentality. The cafeteria age rejoices in the love of love, of emotion, and of intuition in contrast to the rational and considered values of the technocratic, achievement-oriented past. The popular success of gothic romances, science-fiction movies, and catastrophe films speaks to an age that prefers sensations and experience to thoughts and judgments. Many of the current fads encourage the development of these traits. The mental health movement emphasizes personal growth and discovery. Gothic romances exist in a fantasy world never duplicated in reality but one inhabited by its readers regularly. The immediate experience with no thought of consequences influences cocaine users as well as marijuana users and alcohol drinkers.

All of the romantic traits encouraged by the popular media and mental therapy groups address themselves generally to the leisure-time sector of the American's life. They seek the time, interest, and money of their audience during their nonworking hours. In this sense, the romantic peddlers encourage the development of healthy or unhealthy schizophrenia in their audience. While at work, the young and old American continues to abide by the rules of reason, discipline, self-denial, and training. The worker operates within the rules of the work place, defers to authority, and generally obeys the reasonable dictates of the work experience. But after work, the romantic cafeteria purveyors take over and encourage the person to be spontaneous and unrestrained. Fewer and fewer people invest work with the interest or energy that they give to their leisure activities. The disco business of the 1970s, open every night of the week, invited everyone to dance. The Charley perfume commercial on television portrayed a no-nonsense businesswoman who shed her business togs in the evening, put on some Charley, got into a sexy outfit, and was ready for a night on the town.

Our culture, thanks to the commercial promoters, is creating a carefree personality while not denying the worker personality for eight hours a day. In so doing, they are shaping a new, eclectic personality, a personality with two different, at times diametrically opposed, characteristics. This is a new departure for Americans. In the past, leisure-time and athletic activities modeled their value system after the work world: rules operated, competition was encouraged, and victory was heralded. Both participants and spectators abided by the rationale of the game. Thus, there was no conflict in personality traits.

The current interest in experiential activities that de-emphasize goals, victories, and evaluation encourage active participation; an alternative value system is developing. Jogging and "social" tennis, for example, stress the value of enjoyment, participation, and sociability rather than the traditional goal of winning. Marketers strive for more and more dancers, record buyers, joggers, and sailors. In 1978, Americans spent $180 billion on their amusements. Personal pleasure became the highest good.

It is only in a culture where the cafeteria mentality prevails that one can encounter individuals who seek therapy to gain insight into their personality while taking drugs that blur consciousness. It is only in a culture that values everything equally, and in so doing, values nothing, that gothic thrillers receive the same attention as literary masterpieces. Just as it is immaterial whether a buyer chooses one leafy salad over another in the cafeteria line, so it seems immaterial whether one spends time reading trivia or the classics. Choices only mean something when they operate within a value framework. If there is no way to judge or compare worth in food, taste, occupation, learning, or religion, then all entries are parceled out in the indiscriminate marketplace as equals.

Anthropologist Clifford Geertz has written: "Eclecticism is self-defeating not because there is only one direction in which it is useful to move, but because there are so many;

it is necessary to choose."[27] The developing cafeteria personality is never required to choose one course of action, any course of action, since one can add or subtract values, attitudes, behaviors with casual abandon. There is never a determining commitment in any direction; rather an amoral experimenting with equally valued (or valueless) activities. Significant material changes, wrought by humans for their mutual benefit, have created unforeseen consequences. Compulsory schooling fulfilled American values, hopes, and beliefs; that is why it gained wide cultural support. But the results of extending public education for more and more years could not be anticipated. New actions and attitudes only come into being when there is a congruence, a harmony between the people and the direction of change. Americans participate in, shape, and encourage the development of the cafeteria approach to life because they share that view of the world; they find it manageable, workable, and feasible to divide up reality, a myriad of phenomena, and a confusion of views into small, discernible units. The cafeteria approach accurately reflects their perspective of life.

It has been the twentieth-century task, ambition, and arrogance to control the physical environment, understand the universe, and promise eternal happiness to all of its inhabitants. No other century has ever promised so much to so many. Americans have been the primary articulators of the promise, the ultimate imperialists of control. It is a promise and a wish that the planet has adopted because it is an essential human wish to understand the environment, to control it, and to predict the future. It is the utopian human wish given shape and direction in the United States. Because of its allure, its universal appeal, and its irresistible features, the cafeteria trend appears irreversible in America, and eventually, in the world.

The American of the twenty-first century, the leader unto the other nations, will cherish the appearance of perpetual youth; all adults will intermingle in the leisure-time activities offered by the marketers. No sooner will a new fad, fashion, or pop culture hero be heralded than all age groups will embrace it, or him/her. The traditional family will lose more and more of its qualities. Rather than generational conflict describing the future family, the generations will occupy the same territory temporarily. Sometimes they will share the same interests; otherwise people will choose their particular amusement from the infinite cafeteria of choices. Children will view their parents as the amateurs, never the professionals, in deciding career choices and in solving emotional problems. Guidance counselors, psychiatrists, and professional coaches will provide the aid, the wisdom, and the answers.

The youth culture, extending for longer and longer periods of time for more and more people, will be the arena in which the individual searches for self. Further, the youth culture will flourish and provide the temporary answers to perpetual youth, a bewildering, enticing, seemingly endless cafeteria. In this anchorless, rudderless world, both old and new anchors will be discovered and will temporarily provide some continuity, and predictability, for the lives of cafeteria Americans—until a new cafeteria opens with more delectable promises.

Chapter

5

American Women as Cafeteria Americans

American women grew up in the 1960s. Though at least two, and possibly three, generations of them were chronologically over eighteen years old, they experienced an amazing and dramatic maturing in the age of rhetorical liberation. They came of age in the sense that they acquired a new self-image and social image, a new view of who they were and how they were to spend the rest of their lives. Indeed, among the ironic consequences of liberation philosophy, extended schooling, longer life, and fewer children, have been American women's interpretations of the new

An early version of this chapter appeared as the final chapter in my second edition of *Herstory: A Record of the American Woman's Past* (1981).

messages. They began to return to college in large, unprecedented numbers; they reentered and/or entered the job market, they lobbied for new laws to end discrimination against their sex, and they adopted the ideology of liberation.

For American women, the 1960s ushered in their revolution, their awakening, and their new traumas. They had always been at the heart of the family, at the center of social life. But now, the effects of compulsory schooling, advanced industrialization, birth-control technology, urban living, and generational conflicts transformed their lives, and slowly changed their attitudes and values. The words of the emancipation ideology took on a personal, amazingly appropriate meaning to them. Many American women came to realize that they had been living a paradox: the culture had proclaimed them esteemed wives and mothers while that same culture provided no real respect for their traditional role. Two generations of American women were particularly susceptible to the words of liberation: the thirty- to forty-year-old college educated women whose children were all in school and who wondered what their educations had been for, and the college and high school women who identified with the civil rights and antiwar movements and transferred their idealism and their energy to the women's liberation movement.

The ideology of the 1960s was based on the old philosophy of individualism, a philosophy never addressed to women before. Women's adult lives had always centered upon the family, never upon the individual. "All men are created equal," rugged individualism, the pioneer spirit were all indigenous American beliefs that referred to male enterprises, male activists, and male qualities. Individual accomplishment meant male accomplishment. In the new, breathtakingly exciting and confusing atmosphere of the youth revolution of the 1960s, individualism was recast to include women, youth, American Indians, Chicanos, and sundry other minorities heretofore not included in the American panoply of equality.

The new material environment mixed with the new ideology of individual liberation was too powerful a combination for women to resist. Women began separating themselves from their husbands, fathers, and children. They started to define themselves and to forge identities apart from their families, a heretofore unknown phenomenon. This lethal combination of forces also won the attention of the new advertisers. American women became a prime market for the new consumer goods. Since the 1920s, they had been the major household shoppers and in the 1960s and 1970s, they were being asked to purchase every new convenience, every new hobby, and every new fad. American women and American youth became the targets for the new commitment to buy, exchange, throw away, and alter goods, services, and life-styles.

Precisely at the same time American women were told they had a right to individual happiness, they faced a world with fewer and fewer adult jobs worth doing; precisely at the same time that they were told to define themselves in a new way, the cafeteria mentality of the ever accommodating marketers bombarded them with new identities, new perishable fashions, and new fragile selves. The traditional values of hard work, of education, and of achievement no longer applied to the post-industrial world of now and the future. American women therefore became the cafeteria personalities writ large; they, with youths, became the major experimenters of new sports, new activities, and new values.

There is a plasticity, a carte blanche quality evident in many American women today. They resemble unformed children, unsure of their future. Thus, they are particularly vulnerable to the cafeteria's message. Many women have rejected the old views and are bewildered. They have few viable alternatives. They are groping for new forms, new behaviors, new values that express their wishes and needs. In all cultures, identity is forged within a cultural framework. It is the family, religion, and all other powerful forces that shape individual identity. As discussed earlier, most of those traditional networks have fallen by the wayside and lost their power and influence to the peculiar new forces of the twentieth century. It is within this changing, valueless context that women must create themselves anew. They must grow up *after* they have reached chronological adulthood. Many sellers compete for their attention, their dollars, and their loyalty. They are being told to base a new life on the thought: if it feels good, do it.

All American women, of course, are not affected by the cafeteria mentality in the same way or in any way at all. Some women, of course, are grown-up, mature, and sure of themselves. There are a number of social types, definable identities, if you will, evident in American life: the "traditional" woman, the "autonomous" woman, the "self-actualized" woman, and the "cafeteria" woman. The traditional woman defines herself in terms of her husband and children. In her youth she dreamt about the wonderful man she would marry and the wonderful home she would have. Fashion designer Edith Head gave advice to her in *How to Dress for Success:*

The you we're talking about is not alone. She is manufactured by the dozens, the hundreds, the thousands, in all sizes and shapes of women, all after success. . . . And in this competitive race, it is frequently the best "packaging" that makes the difference between those who are sought after and snapped up fast in the well-stocked supermarket of modern life.[1]

Edith Head's language accurately depicts the market perspective of the marriageable woman. She is in a competitive race. She must be properly packaged and quickly picked up; otherwise, she will be the dreaded outdated product, last year's model in a new, increasingly desperate market. Marabel Morgan's best-seller *The Total Woman* was the

1970s equivalent of Edith Head's advice book. Making the proper martini, asking the hubby the right question, and dressing appropriately for the cocktail hour were Morgan's practical tips for a woman aiming to preserve her successful marriage, or to give new excitement to a boring one.

The traditional woman has always existed in America. Indeed, she had been the majority until the 1960s. Little girls were raised with the belief that their adult destiny centered upon marriage and a family. Mothers trained daughters in the domestic arts; only a small minority, often pitied by their contemporaries, remained unmarried adults and they were called spinsters, solitary women spinning yarn in someone else's household. Though many women questioned the restrictions placed upon adult women's lives, only the brave few openly challenged or defied society. The women abolitionists, temperance workers, and feminists of the nineteenth century were among the brave few who did. But the culture offered few possibilities and no enticements for adult women to define themselves as other than wives and mothers. That remained for the twentieth century to accomplish.

The autonomous woman is the career-oriented woman who is willing to reject the traditional woman's values and life goals to achieve success in a man's world. The autonomous woman takes and leaves men in the way that men have traditionally used and misused women. The autonomous woman claims liberation to be based upon her absolute autonomy, her independence of all people. She is emotionally and intellectually free of all ties, an adventurer in a man's marketplace, a competitive racerunner who cherishes the race and the victory. The autonomous woman has essentially accepted the male success model. She becomes as driven in her business pursuits or her professional career as any man; she devotes herself to her own advancement with equal ruthlessness. She is a public woman, a woman whose life is lived outside the domestic sphere but according to the traditional male rules of the marketplace game.

The autonomous woman has also existed throughout American history, but until recently she was a rarity, an exception that usually proved the rule. Because she was unusual, she could not pass on to the next generation the lessons she had learned from her experiences. Social structures were not created to accommodate her; parents did not wish for their daughters to emulate her. The public world remained largely a male world and women who ventured into it ran the considerable risk of being labeled mannish, the kiss of death in our culture. Until recently, then, autonomous women were the rebellious few, the unusual exceptions in each generation, of society's view of women.

The self-actualized woman, the successful eclectic, is a self-respecting female who has preserved a rich interaction with others while fulfilling her own personal needs and goals. She no longer lives exclusively for others but she interprets her life as one that is inextricably tied to others. She may be married, have a family and a career; she may be a working-class woman who has only invested a minimum of herself in her work, thereby reserving energy and interest in her family, her community, her church, and her friends. She may be a middle-class woman, experienced in volunteer work, whose sources of gratification include her organization, her family, her home, and her friends. The self-actualized woman, whose network of life involves people in a reciprocal relationship of concern, may well become the psychically whole leaders of the next generation.

The essential ingredient that the self-actualized woman possesses is self-respect, not narcissism and not arrogance, but true respect for her own worth and her own potential. Joan Didion, in an essay entitled "On Self-Respect" has described the trait thusly: "The dismal fact is that self-respect has nothing to do with the approval of others – who are, after all, deceived easily enough – has nothing to do with reputation, which, as Rhett Butler told Scarlett O'Hara, is something people with courage can do without."[2] Self-respecting women do not gauge their lives by the dictates of others. Surely authority figures such as parents, clergy, and teachers participate in shaping the female personality, but in contrast to the traditional woman who carved her life according to social values of the "others," the self-actualized woman sifts and chooses the various options open to all humans and creates a self with which she is comfortable. She can do this precisely because she is respectful of her own wishes, of her own judgments, and of her own goals. "People with self-respect exhibit a certain toughness, a kind of moral nerve; they display what was once called character, a quality which, although approved in the abstract, sometimes loses ground to other, more instantly negotiable virtues."[3] Didion's description is particularly difficult for women to achieve. Our culture does not encourage women to have nerve, to be tough, and to have an independent character. Yet this is the essential trait needed to achieve self-actualized womanhood status. Against enormous odds, some self-actualized women already exist, indeed have always existed.

The cafeteria woman picks and chooses values, behaviors, and activities almost with the same thoughtfulness that she chooses which salad to eat in the cafeteria. She has rejected the traditional value structure and the male success model but has found no adequate substitute. She knows what she does not want to be, but she does not know what she is or wishes to be. While young, she indulges in adolescent rebellious behavior that is understood as such, and is therefore assumed to be temporary. However, she never moves beyond the adolescent behavior. She continues to experiment, to wear ideas like clothes, to discard them casually, to try some new line of pursuit, some new drug, and some new dance with the same casual abandon. She has trouble making decisions because she has no solid measure by which to choose. Her methods of evaluation are superficial, poorly formed by media advertisers, heroes, and slogans. Her view of life is an abbreviated form of the *Reader's Digest,* a digest of a digest. The fewer words, thoughts, ideas, the better. She is doomed to experiment in the infinite variety of cafeterias forever.

Traditional women are able to withstand amazing social changes, confident in their belief that their social role is also a personally satisfying one. Autonomous women are products of increased educational opportunities for women, the ideology of modern feminism, and the economic necessities of late twentieth-century life. They are the first substantial group of career women who came of age in the 1970s. The self-actualized women are the minority of women who have been able to create a wise and healthy synthesis between the traditional and innovative roles for women.

In sharp contrast to all of these other social types, the cafeteria woman is the female adolescent adult, the natural companion to the perpetual male adolescent. Both represent the emerging eclectic personality of the late twentieth century. They never grow up. They never choose life courses but rather change jobs, roles, and values according to whim. They do not have the structures of religion or the family to provide them with both boundaries and nourishment. School and play, both based upon the cafeteria model, govern their lives.

While the traditional woman is the most familiar to us and the self-actualized woman the most difficult type to achieve, the autonomous woman, the public woman, has had a long but tortuous history in this country. She has sometimes been a woman professional. But who is she? Is she a new kind of adult who combines traditional roles with new ones? Is she an imitator of men? Or is she simply aberrant? In the cafeteria that is America, people are given the impression that they can select a variety of roles and create their own synthesis. Ideally, then, women should be able to carve an adult identity in which the professional self is integrated into a personality that already contains culturally learned female roles. She should not have to relinquish the traditional roles to attain the new one.

But reality is not ideal. Given the long-held cultural

views about women's adult destiny as wives and mothers, women who ventured into the public world of work encountered many unconscious and conscious obstacles. Historically, they have been more successful in areas of work that did not originally require professional training: as writers, teachers, nurses, and entertainers. When they entered developed professional fields that were already dominated by men, they found it difficult, if not impossible, to succeed. If they succeeded, it was according to the male values, standards, and styles already in place. They never became women professionals in a way that made the word "women" an adjective, as descriptive of their unique blending of their "femaleness" and their professionalism.

According to the sociological literature, a social type consists of a group of individuals who consciously share a number of characteristics. In the case of the professional as a social type, the members belong to the same organizations, have the same education, and the same set of goals. They agree to a set of rules that govern their professional behavior and generally absorb the style befitting their particular profession. Women professionals, particularly those in male dominated professions, have traditionally identified with their professions; they have accepted the male defined rules for proper behavior as chemist, lawyer, doctor, or engineer. A woman's "femaleness" has never become a participating factor in her self-definition as a professional nor did it appear, except as a barrier to overcome, in the eyes of the male professional.

If women have been acculturated differently from men (an accepted truism in this country), their upbringing and experience should be different from men's. It would follow logically that their behavior, their values, and their style would also differ markedly. Women doctors, for example, might exhibit more human compassion, more concern with establishing a personal relationship with the patient, and more sensitivity to subtle personality differences than male doctors. This difference in behavior would not come because women were biologically more sensitive or humane, but because their female culture was based upon concern for others and interaction with family members. A woman lawyer might be better as a negotiator than as a trial lawyer since her upbringing required her to get along with her siblings, help her mother, and, if she herself were a mother, act as an arbitrator in family disputes.

Women doctors and lawyers, if they consciously brought their female culture to their professional life, could effect enormous changes on their respective professions. Instead, each generation of women lawyers, doctors, and scientists has had to surmount the male barriers, learn the male rules, and operate within an externally determined male environment. Once women entered the awesome profession, they abided by the male rituals. That is why the history of women professionals in America is often a history of each generation beginning anew; the links between the generations, the transferring of traditions among women professionals, has been absent. A chasm rather than a chain connects the generations. The obstacles surmounted by the first generation of women doctors in the midnineteenth century still need surmounting in the late twentieth century. A woman professional generally accepted the profession's definition of what its members should be, and she effected a healthy schizophrenia: she was a woman in her private life and a "professional," defined by the males, in her public life. The two selves were separate and distinct.

In a sense, the few women who ventured into medicine prior to the 1970s accepted their femaleness within a male profession by following the established view that women doctors should specialize in "women's" areas: pediatrics, psychiatry, obstetrics, and gynecology. By assenting to this segregation within the profession however, they were conceding without a fight to the dominant male view that women were naturally better suited to these specialties. There was no discussion of female culture. Women engineers and architects were notably absent in large construction projects; women designers beautified interiors but did not build bridges.

Even when women doctors, in a defensive effort, organized their own group within the profession, they usually devoted themselves to "womanly" topics—prevention of children's diseases, public health, and preventive medicine. Rarely did they agitate for the removal of restrictions upon women's admittance to medical schools or complain vociferously about the absence of women in surgery. The women's medical organizations did not become a support facility for women in the profession or an active recruiter of women candidates. Neither did they alter the medical style or tone shaped by male doctors. These actions, or lack of them, can best be understood as evidence of the women professionals' failure as a social type. Most women professionals did not believe in women's total equality within their field; they viewed themselves as special, rare, and unique.

American culture has encouraged the view of women professionals as special, or more likely, as aberrant. The successful woman careerist/homemaker is a rare breed and one rarely encouraged in tradition-bound America. Thus, it is no surprise that when women defy the stereotypes and enter medical school and struggle through the trial by fire known as a medical education, they have totally accepted the rules of the profession and have no desire to "rock the boat." Often they are tortured by their uniqueness, their rebellion against cultural expectations, and wonder whether they are queer or unusual in marking an atypical path for themselves. If they successfully combine a career with marriage and motherhood, they assume they are extraordinarily lucky and/or talented and that their experience cannot be emulated. They also may become part of the newer social type, the self-actualized woman.

Since professionalization began in the United States, raising standards in medical and legal training has always meant discriminating against women. As states began licensing their professionals and schools raised their requirements for entry as well as their length of study, no serious discussion ensued as to how to reconcile these new strictures with a woman's life. Since most women married and became mothers at a young age, how could they conform to the lengthy preparations for a profession? The unspoken assumption was that professions were designed only for men. It is only in the 1980s that this path is being taken more frequently by increasing numbers of women. If they remain single and childless, they will remain autonomous women. If they marry, have children, and continue to pursue a career actively, they will enter the ranks of the self-actualized woman, the rarest social type of all.

How do you create large numbers of self-respecting, self-actualized women? How do you develop little girls into grown women who cherish their uniqueness, their opinions, their personalities, and their right to be? How do you convince mothers and fathers that there is more than one adult scenario for all women? How, indeed, do you cultivate oneness at the same time that you teach social responsibility? These are mighty questions, questions that are at the heart of the issue, for it is self-respecting girls who will become self-respecting women with identities that merge the best of individual and social needs.

The intense questioning of cultural values resulting from the women's movement has already gotten some young women to reject their social definition. The growing numbers of young women who remain single, who marry and remain childless, and who declare their preference for homosexuality all represent breakaways from the old rules. They voice in the loudest terms possible, by their behavior, a rejection of traditional values. Some of these women become autonomous women, as already suggested, driving careerists who sacrifice their personal life for their profession. Some develop a healthy balance between private wishes and public responsibilities. Some women have moved from dependence to independence to healthy interdependence, and in so doing have achieved self-actualization.

Official discrimination against women has been legally prohibited, but the most important change resulting from the women's movement is the shift in attitudes and behavior on everyone's part. Bold parents are testing the new feminism, living in egalitarian marriages, and sharing in child raising. Adolescent girls are questioning their traditional parents' expectations for them and grown women are going through analysis, breaking down and breaking through their traditional roles, while seeking new forms of selfhood.

The critics of women's liberation, like the critics of the suffrage movement, perceive the truly revolutionary nature of the movement. They recognize that feminism leads directly to the reorganization of the human family and to the questioning of established social patterns. They realize that self-respecting women may not choose the socially approved script for all women. Marabel Morgan's best-seller *The Total Woman* and Phyllis Schlafly's anti-ERA campaign mounted a frontal attack upon women's liberation. They aggressively defended the status quo, aware of the multiple dangers of the enemy. The best defense is an offense, and Morgan and Schlafly surely utilized this tactic. They spoke for some middle- and upper-class white women who enjoyed the privileged position of homemaker; they decried the liberationist's wish for all women to discover and develop their talents, skills, and ambitions. To Morgan and Schlafly, the home, husband, and family demanded the woman's full-time attention. While women's liberation, in its best form, represented the self-actualized woman, the Schlafly model defended the traditional woman and argued that the woman's liberation movement had as its goal the autonomous woman.

This point deserves elaboration. The traditional ideal was a self-sacrificing, self-effacing woman who devoted her energies to others. She worked for her husband's and family's happiness, always deferring her desires. If they were all happy, she would be happy; so ran the rationale. A mother's primary goal was one of self-sacrifice, and thousands of fictional melodramas and soap operas gained adherents because of this fundamental premise. The autonomous woman, in contrast, rejected others in her wholehearted search for self. She forgot, or willingly gave up, her connections with family and friends to pursue her professional goals and to achieve success in the public arena. The self-actualized woman had achieved a self-respecting self and combined the best of traditional and autonomous womanhood. She balanced the authentic relationships treasured by the traditional woman with her personal needs for self-fulfillment in areas other than the family. She combined the personal, the traditional, and the public.

Fundamentally, the crux of the controversy centers around the question: For whom should women live? For themselves or for others? Western culture emphasizes the others in a woman's life as taking priority over her own wishes and dreams, while feminism proclaims the importance of her wishes. Though the American dream has always included individual will, in reality the dream has only had a male expression. In an age when the basic values of America are being questioned, women's liberation harmonizes with the goals of the discontented, the underprivileged, the young, and the powerless. While white males have had both a social and an individual definition, women, blacks, children, and American Indians have only had a social definition. Society decided who they were, what they could have, and how they would live their lives.

Morgan, Schlafly, and other critics of women's liberation believed that the social definition of woman was the proper, holy, and desired one. They were puzzled and outraged by the efforts to change that definition. While rugged individualism and a variety of adult roles were appropriate for males, all women shared the same destiny. Marriage, the pleasures of a home, husband, and children, remained the central focus of all women's lives. For Morgan and Schlafly, the status quo represented the best of all possible worlds for women and only the maladjusted and perverted sought change. The critics of women's liberation never asked why marriage was not the central focus of a man's life.

While most men never achieve the material rewards of this culture and do not feel that they had innumerable adult life choices, until recently, women were not even included in the rhetoric or the dream. It is only by struggling against all odds that women freed themselves of cultural definitions and embarked upon unchartered courses. For women who do not accept society's definition of them, the way is unpredictable, difficult, and traumatic. They must carve their own identities, their own defenses, their own strengths.

Every generation has had its heroic women challengers, its self-actualized women. But in this generation, there is the important support of the women's movement and the even more significant phenomenon of the new sociological reality for urban, industrial, middle-class American women. Contrary to Morgan and Schlafly, there are fewer constructive tasks associated with homemaker than ever before. A frontier woman raised children and chickens, grew vegetables, put up preserves, cooked over an open fire, sewed the clothes for the whole family, taught the children how to read, and cleaned the cabin daily. She had no refrigerator, sewing machine, running water, toilet facility, ready-made clothes, or canned food. The homemaker role was a functional, sixteen-hour-a-day job. Today, that is no longer the case, though manufacturers of home appliances, gadgets, and other paraphernalia try to occupy the woman for endless hours. A frontier woman baked her own bread out of necessity; a 1980s housewife bakes bread to give her "fulfillment," a sorry indication that the useful functions of her role no longer exist.

Days without events, children who no longer need constant attention, and a busy husband contribute to the creation of questioning women. The woman's movement provides emotional support as well as concrete suggestions so that women can direct their energies into constructive outlets. The whole society demonstrates its adaptive qualities in responding to this new population. Universities, losing enrollment from the diminishing numbers of eighteen-year-olds, promote continuing education programs and establish university extensions in the suburbs; private child care facilities increase; and professional schools encourage female applicants. Adult women today ask questions and consider answers that previously were the domain of eighteen- and twenty-two-year-olds exclusively. They join the adolescent generation in wondering what they will do with their lives.

The scenario for the woman's future is exciting and dangerous. The thrill of unpredictability, of testing new dreams, and of seeking self-definitions will be mixed with the dangers of unforeseen obstacles, failures, and conflicted wishes. Many women will attempt a synthesis for their adult life, a good American eclectic mixture of home, family, and outside interests and in so doing, become self-actualized women. A significant minority will become full-time careerists, autonomous women, who may or may not marry and have children. Some will continue in the traditional woman's world. The nuclear family, I think, will remain the primary social institution in which children will be raised and men and women will live together. People will continue having children, though in fewer numbers.

If the cafeteria mentality captures the woman while she is still young and impressionable, there is a real possibility that she will be arrested in this stage of development for the rest of her life. Since all youth, as described earlier, are segregated into their own subculture and are required to gain nourishment and sustenance only from one another, they define themselves in ways that seem appropriate to their adolescent minds but are really not appropriate for adult life. They suffer from what Erik Erickson calls "adolescent plasticity." Their emphasis upon immediate pleasure, upon variety for its own sake, upon action over thoughtfulness, and upon perpetual youthful activity makes them particularly susceptible to the cafeteria mentality, a mentality fed and encouraged by the sellers of America. Young women, searching for self-definition, an activity they share with young men, but with the added burden of reckoning with the traditional, time-honored definition of women, may fall prey to the delicious temptations of this cafeteria mentality and give up the search for self before they truly engage in it.

The emerging cafeteria woman is sometimes a tragic figure, sometimes a thoughtless one. She may be torn between self-gratification and social involvement, thereby qualifying her for tragedy. Or she may be unaware of the fluid nature of her self, of the perpetually unfinished quality of her identity. The unhappy cafeteria woman recognizes the competing demands and needs; she has not been able to take advantage of the new promises and activities while fulfilling the old obligations. The eclectic merger falls apart; it is too fragile, self-contradictory, and tense. The inconsistencies and internal self-doubts are too great. She is one of the victims of sudden change, of fads overtaking thoughtful and sometimes painful adjustment.

I am afraid that the cafeteria woman will proliferate and overtake the self-actualized woman as the dominant model for future women. Beginning as a part of the faddish youth group, women will continue to behave in the temporary, quickly changing mode of youths. They will change husbands, life-styles, hobbies, and values as quickly as will the cafeteria men with whom they will live. They will accept the individualistic philosophy, the pleasure principle, and the value of experience over insight that characterizes the youth culture and its eager market suppliers. In truly dialectical terms, though, the very breathless changes that characterize this type will produce its opposite: a traditional, return-to-the-past personality, a lover of history and the good old days. The eternal youth and eternally young men and women of the future will produce diametrically opposite personality structures as well as new syntheses, new blends with which to begin the bewildering cycle all over again.

The anchorless, unsatisfied, and unsatisfying heroine of much popular fiction today appropriately symbolizes the cafeteria woman. She knows what she is against but she does not know what she is for. She is in perpetual motion, having rejected all the traditional sources of rootedness. The cafeteria heroine of contemporary fiction finds herself in the company of older, more traditional heroines. One of the important features of cafeteria America is the simultaneous presence of contradictory types; so the restless fictional heroine finds herself located on the shelf next to the suffering, yearning romantic heroine of yesteryear. In an age of liberation and individualism, gothic romances, for example, continue to sell very well. With more women working than ever before, paperback publishers delight in their sales of Barbara Cartland romances and television producers gloat in the success of their nighttime and daytime soap operas.

Because the cafeteria makes no judgments, it offers seemingly contradictory offerings simultaneously. So women readers and viewers are regaled with romance and melodrama, with traditional heroines and working-class wives. Obviously, some human need is being satisfied if so many women consume so much of this genre. Indeed, one could argue that the cafeteria mentality accounts for all human taste and therefore never overlooks any human anxiety or need. It is truly a democratic impulse.

American women emerge from their popular cultural experiences with seemingly multiple images; but this impression is false. The authentic choices are limited in this cafeteria. Women have few choices that offer guidelines for new roles or values; none are grounded in a clearly defined set of principles. Romance or independence may not be desirable alternatives. The way popular cultural representatives frame the issues denies true choice and freedom. Similarly, there is no exploration of social needs, communal standards, and traditional customs as sources of knowledge or guidance. Within the woman's dilemma is also contained the dilemma of all Americans drawn to the cafeteria mode of living. There is no way to judge the alternatives. The vacuum called individual is expected to select first one cafeteria offering and then another.

True to the cafeteria, however, and despite my fears, the traditional, autonomous, self-actualized, and cafeteria woman will probably coexist in the twenty-first century. Indeed, she will exchange traits, values, identities, and behavior, each with the other, and create uneasy, inconsistent connections that will temporarily prevail, only to be replaced with newer and more novel possibilities.

Chapter

6

Popular Culture: The Supreme Cafeteria

If the older generations no longer lead the younger ones, and if women are being initiated into the vacuum of endless choices, there are few directions, few guideposts for Americans to follow. Surely the American commitment to choice offers no frame of reference; religious and reform subcultural institutions become the few hopeful roads for many to seek and follow. And so they do. But the overwhelming engagement of Americans is with the arena of popular entertainments. Most people seek amusement, explanation, and meaning in popular culture. It is here that they receive their images of human behavior and its values. Clint Eastwood shows us how to stand up for ourselves, the women on "Dynasty" offer the possible roles for women, and all situation comedies teach us that life's crises will be resolved with laughter. Popular culture is no longer confined to escapism or amusement, rather it offers edification and meaning for many lives.

Because the many offerings of popular culture change regularly, with short life spans being their typical fate, Americans are used to variety and to change. Television, the premier medium of the electronic age, is omnipresent. Longevity, in a performer or a program, is observed with wonder. Lucille Ball's multigenerational television career, John Wayne's and Cary Grant's long movie careers, and Elizabeth Taylor's survivability as a celebrity offer audiences examples of exceptions to the dominant rule; they survived, indeed, persevered, in the sea of constant change called popular culture. They also appealed most to the older generations, the over-forty Americans who are enjoying longer and longer lives, but who grew up during a less changing, less frantic environment of popular entertainments.

Another feature of late twentieth-century popular culture is its resemblance to the business and the education worlds that share the same goal: selling their product to as large an audience as possible. While entertainments have always been with us, when they combined in the twentieth century with sophisticated communications technologies and the latest in so-called scientific marketing methods, they became omnipresent and omnipotent. Americans' continual interest in amusement, in variety, and in increasing leisure-time activities interacted with the highly profitable business of show business. Entertainment became a highly commercial enterprise while the business world sought to sell its wares by using entertainers and entertainments.

The boundaries between the three institutions blurred, if they did not disappear. Educators used advertising and marketing techniques to attract students and tried to highlight both the pleasurable dimensions of learning along with the pragmatic benefits. Little or nothing was said of hard work, discipline, and frustration. Lawyers and accountants became the chief executives of movie studios and television networks. All agreed that continual expansion of America's cafeteria of goods, services, and amusements was inherently worthwhile. Everyone profited in some way in this interchangeable universe.

It all began with vaudeville, one of the earliest and most successful forms of twentieth-century American popular culture. Indeed, it epitomizes the American hunger for the cafeteria, for seemingly endless choices presented in an entertaining and speedy fashion. Vaudeville gave audiences of the first three decades of this century a chance to experience different forms of amusement in two hours. The classic vaudeville show consisted of nine acts. The acrobats were followed by a song-and-dance team, a revue, a comedy routine, a jazz band, an intermission, a good musician, a sketch, a strong comedy single, and an animal act. Americans delighted in the fast-paced, diverse presentation. They became accustomed to changing routines, new stars, new songs, and new fashions. Old routines were booed off the stage and newness was applauded.

The vaudeville show exemplifies a trend that was to continue, accelerate, and dominate the American psyche in the twentieth century. It captured the diversity of immigrant America; it flourished among ethnic audiences. Both the WASP public and the immigrants were presented with bits of exotica and esoterica from various subcultures, mixed with the tried and true formula entertainments. All tastes would be satisfied. Entertainers with wider appeal performed before more diverse audiences. The market principle applied in vaudeville. Fanny Brice began in a local Brooklyn vaudeville house but succeeded to Broadway. Indeed, Broadway and then Hollywood became the golden hope for all entertainers. Audiences decided whether they would get there. To satisfy the quest for novelty, producers offered audiences newer, bigger, and better choices with each new show.

Within vaudeville, three determining elements of popular culture could be found, elements that epitomized the cafeteria approach to life: (1) a bewildering assortment of amusements with no internal unity or consistency; (2) pseudochoices presented in the guise of authentic choices; and (3) *divertissment* that discouraged serious thinking or analysis. Though audiences could be, and often were, critical of inept dancers or comedians, they could not evaluate a dancer relative to a singer, or a comedian to a serious actor. Vaudeville implicitly expected its audiences to withhold judgment of the whole and to see each part as discreet and separate. The viewer could judge a single act but not the whole, since there was no coherent whole. In this way, vaudeville contributed to the compartmentalization of American life, an important aspect of the cafeteria approach.

Because vaudeville offered pseudochoices, audiences truly had no choices. There were not that many kinds, styles, genres presented, but the impression conveyed was that yes, indeed, the audience had a wide variety of choices. Most entertainments came in formulaic packages; the western, the romance, and the comedy, based on classical forms, took on peculiarly American traits. By the twentieth century, other kinds of adventure stories had replaced the western as the most popular type, but the essential ingredients with the hero overcoming the villain and saving the heroine remained intact. Americans enjoyed the repetitions of their popular entertainments and usually rejected any major departures. In this sense, they collaborated with the producers of their amusements. Some popular singers, for example, may have been prettier than others, but they usually conformed to the prevailing taste of beauty, and they all sang songs with lyrics that offered conventional wisdom.

Since popular culture's offerings were designed to amuse and divert, audiences were not expected to analyze, dissect, or consider its serious meaning. Americans did not discuss popular novels nor did they analyze the significance of a vaudeville show. They suspended evaluation and in so doing became less and less able to make distinctions in other areas of their lives. The essence of more and more products of the amusement factory was its perishability. Thus, no one was encouraged to contemplate or comment on something that had such a brief life. Tomorrow was another show, another song, another TV night.

Vaudeville and its successors taught Americans to visualize the world as unconnected. By denying connections between acts, the first step is taken toward the uncoupling of values, of behaviors, and of identities. All actions lose context and meaning; they simply are. Because little is invested in the amusement, little is lost if it proves boring or difficult. Human relationships also are judged according to this non-criterion. If the partner is not regularly amusing, then the partner is to be discarded. Since the video world of the 1980s changes its images rapidly, the level of patience and tolerance is very low. One should not be required to wait long periods of time for the event, the person, or the story to explain itself, amuse others, or happily resolve the problem. The presentation of cafeterialike choices in all aspects of American culture strongly suggests to the consumer that everything can be sampled, and if the buyer is dissatisfied, the item can be returned or discarded without penalty or consequence.

Two of popular culture's biggest musical stars in the 1980s effectively symbolize the confusion arising from the cafeteria approach to life. Prince and Michael Jackson, both adored by black and white preteens (precisely the audience who screamed for Elvis Presley and the Beatles), present themselves as androgynous, both masculine and feminine in their physical and psychological traits. While Prince sang lyrics with decidedly sexual meanings, he appeared on the stage, according to one description, "in high-heeled boots, a flouncy ruffled blouse and a purple quasi-Edwardian suit. . . ."[1] He walked across the stage " . . . taking long strides that end in a hiplocking sway, a Rita Hayworth sort of walk."[2]

Prince projected the image of a bisexual whose appearance suggested the feminine side of him. He stopped granting interviews because he said, he contradicted himself too often.[3] The sexual content of his songs contained no moral message, no standard by which to measure behavior. Do what feels good; do not do whatever is uncomfortable. Audiences seemed to enjoy his outrageous poses and though no one claimed he had a good voice, his record albums and concert appearances were very well received.

Michael Jackson, by contrast, is often portrayed as childlike, as a highly successful performer who gave up his real childhood to sing with his brothers, the Jackson Five, and then to go out on his own to spectacular acclaim. He is described as androgynous in appearance: "On stage in one of his sequined jump suits, he's a flamboyant picture of grace, a sleek jaguar ready to pounce." He is also described as "beguiling, angelic, androgynous."[4] Jackson's songs, however, speak of innocent love and of romance and are not as sexually explicit as Prince's.

But in both cases, the images projected would tend to blur the distinctions between the sexes, blur the categories of differences, and suspend the ability to judge. In this admittedly great leap, I am suggesting that the dramatic contrast between these representatives of 1980s popular music culture and earlier generations' heroes suggests not merely a loosening of social mores, as many commentators have said, but rather a confirmation of this generation's commitment to a no-values value system, a cafeteria of life where anything and everything goes. All sexual behavior is acceptable. None have important consequences.

In 1986, Madonna, another popular teen idol, sang "Papa Don't Preach," in which she asked for her father's support of her pregnancy. She sang vaguely of marrying her lover at a future time, but meanwhile neither her father nor society should judge her actions. Teenage mothers, according to this view, are perfectly capable of assuming the responsibility of motherhood. Once again, part of the cafeteria metaphor seems to inspire this attitude. Sexual activity, as a pleasurable experience, becomes good in itself; pregnancy may or may not result, and somehow it seems unrelated to sexual activity. Teenagers often admit that they had no idea that sexual intercourse might result in pregnancy. They had successfully compartmentalized one behavior so that they saw no connection to others. This is a dramatic example of cafeteria behavior.

Another feature of contemporary America that speaks to the cafeteria theme of variety and change is the makeup of the family or, as the U.S. Census Bureau refers to it, the American household. Twenty-five percent of adult Americans live alone, an historically unprecedented number.[5] The number of female-headed households and childless-couple households are on the rise. Unmarried senior citizens of the opposite sex live together as do homosexual male and lesbian couples. All kinds of new, extended family situations exist.

Obviously, there are important demographic and economic reasons for this, but the ease with which Americans have accepted the astonishing variety of households suggests a gradual perception, in the last twenty years particularly, of change and variety as inherent in all aspects of American life. There is a tolerance for difference in lifestyles (that very term suggests individuality and diversity) that indicates an acceptance of change as a necessity of life. Sameness and continuity bespeak of rigidity and old-fashioned ways. Only unabashed traditionalists assert the past as desirable and authoritative. People of various ages may shake their heads at the variety of new living arrangements, and pride themselves in the fact that they live in a traditional nuclear family, but they shake their heads in silence. After all, at a later stage in their longer life, they may enter into what now appears to them as an unconventional arrangement.

The vaudeville contribution to the cafeteria insures the segregation of each part of life, of each activity, from each other. Living arrangements exist as do work habits and play time, but there is no assumption that the parts unite into a consistent whole. From this point it is a short step to the other ingredients of the cafeteria: the minimal investment, the suspension of judgment, and the willingness to keep choosing new possibilities from the endless cafeteria. The video world of the 1980s, the successor to the vaudeville show, only confirms these tendencies. Television presents its programs in seven minute segments punctuated by commercials that, in themselves, become brief vignettes of America's values. Popular songs last but a few minutes, encapsulated versions of life's messages and patterns.

There is a questing and unfinished quality to cafeteria personalities. Being formed during the vulnerable adolescent years when youths are looking for anchors and evidence of their self-worth, they are confronted with a myriad of choices, each presented as equally good. Also searching for self-definition in the new world of liberation, women are given packaged and processed answers and explanations. Instead of finding coherent and comprehensive guides to self-development, the various marketers of post-industrial America entice both groups with their endless variety of goods, each of which assumes a different set of role expectations. Sellers of sports paraphernalia compete with mental health producers, college admission recruiters, and fads to capture the minds and behavior of American adolescents and women.

The resulting cafeteria person displays the uncanny joining together of many trends in American culture. Compulsory schooling for more people for more years, the ultraspecialization of the work place, the proliferation of consumer goods, the increase in leisure time, and the prolongation of the youth subculture all interact to produce this new personality type. The prevailing ideology is to invest little of yourself in a project, role, or activity and if it does not work out, try something else. The cafeteria offers many choices, none of which require a major investment in time, energy, or commitment. If the salad is not good, then tomorrow you will choose something else to eat. Cafeteria dining is not a significant, time-consuming activity nor are the life possibilities offered to the youthful consumer in cafeteria America. Once vulnerable youths become oriented to the cafeteria mentality, they base their lives upon its dubious premises and within its fragile structure. And since America reveres its young, it imitates the trend toward cafeteria personalities.

American material culture reflects the cafeteria image. Buffet tables, catalogs, multiple-choice examinations, and the shopping mall are only a few examples of the American love of the eclectic, the cafeteria writ large. The sinister factor of the cafeteria enters the scene when the cafeteria becomes the framework, the conception, and the guiding principle for the human personality. It is here that the material, the psyche, and the idea merge to create the plastic American identity.

One learns about oneself, one's strengths and weaknesses, within a cultural and subcultural environment of opportunity. Individuals measure, test, and compare their values and behaviors to the overall culture's. Rebels and critics also find support groups and congenial spirits in diverse American culture. There are few examples of truly un-American behavior. The commitment and circumstance of tolerance and diversity of past generations have become the cafeteria mentality of the present. While young people and women are particularly susceptible to the cafeteria mentality, no one is immune. Neither has any dimension of American life escaped the cafeteria frame of reference.

Historian Laurence Veysey has noted that, "Leisure constantly suggests choice, in contrast to the economic necessities that bound the earlier family."[6] Since Americans work less than earlier generations, and rely heavily upon commercialized entertainments to occupy their leisure hours, choice becomes a self-propelling phenomenon, a constantly changing cafeteria of possibilities. Further, there is a new group of working Americans, called "new collars" by Ralph Whitehead, who base their identities on their leisure-time activities, not on their work. According to a summary of Whitehead's views, the new collars are an important segment of the middle class, people whose jobs are neither blue-collar nor upper-middle professional.[7] The new collars have abandoned the achievement orientation of the traditional American; their self is invested in pleasurable pursuits, not in their work.

If we use my earlier categorization of women and apply it to all Americans, then the new collars become part of the growing cafeteria personality group. They join the impressionable youths, the newly awakened women, and the young professionals of both sexes who yield to the cafeteria impulse in their leisure time. Surely there are members of all of these groups who remain in the traditional category; some are autonomous, while still others are self-actualized, combining the best of the old and new worlds. But the imperialistic feature of the cafeteria escapes only the hardy few. The traditional, autonomous, and self-actualized people who are able to sample the cafeteria's wares while being firmly grounded in a value-based culture and subculture are the greatest beneficiaries.

Because women entered the adult world when the cafeteria had overtaken traditional values, so to speak, they are at a disadvantage. It is harder for them to achieve the self-actualized status where a successful integration of traditional values and career opportunities can be undertaken. Similarly, black Americans of both sexes entered the world of opportunity when the cafeteria was already in full bloom. Many, of course, remain committed to traditional values of religion and family life. Black women, particularly, already demonstrate great interest in education and career while remaining committed to traditional roles for women. The challenge for all Americans is to experience the cafeteria while anchored to a values base.

The reality of the cafeteria metaphor enables traditional people, autonomous people, and self-actualized people to coexist with the large numbers of cafeteria people. Since variety, change, compartmentalization, and relativity are the prevailing values of the cafeteria, traditionalists must be tolerated by cafeteria peoples. There is enough space and enough choices to accommodate everyone. Further, the pull of both the religious and reform subcultures is sufficient to recruit members from all constituencies. Americans join causes and are reborn into Christianity, lose faith and abandon causes with great frequency. Cafeteria personalities enter these subcultures also while experiencing the many riches of popular culture.

Given the basic characteristics of the cafeteria mentality, nothing (no value and no behavior) is mutually exclusive; everything coheres. Therefore, seemingly contradictory traits mingle together in a human personality; only when diametrically opposed values or actions clash within an individual is there breakdown and the inability to function effectively. The success of various mental health therapies may suggest that the parts of the cafeteria personality do not always harmonize or coexist favorably. Of course, traditional, autonomous, and self-actualized personalities may also require help from mental health therapies, but the cafeteria personality seems more vulnerable than the others.

The cafeteria has no moral structure inherent within it. It is an attitude, a material fact, a prevailing mode of modern life that can provide marvelous choices if the choice is based upon a self-conscious, value based philosophy. If not, the chooser is doomed to constant selection, rejection, and selection again. For the anchorless, the riches of America's cafeteria become a never-ending whirl with less and less meaning attached to more and more choices.

NOTES

CHAPTER 1

1. Quoted in A. H. Fromenson, "New York: Amusements and Social Life," in *The Russian Jews in the United States,* edited by Charles S. Bernheimer, 1915 reprint (New York: August M. Kelley, 1971), 229.

2. Quoted in Betty Friedan, "Feminism's Next Step," *The New York Times Magazine,* (July 5, 1981): 32.

3. Christopher Lasch, "The Waning of Private Life," *Salmagundi* 36 (Winter 1977): 6.

CHAPTER 2

1. Randolph S. Bourne, "The Two Generations," *Atlantic Monthly* 107 (May 1911): 592.

2. Ibid., 593.

3. E. G. Stern, *My Mother and I* (New York: Macmillan, 1971).

4. Fannie Hurst, "The Gold in Fish" in *Song of Life* (New York: Alfred A. Knopf, 1927), 63.

5. Ibid., 73–74.

6. Hannah Arendt, "The Crisis in Education," in *Between Past and Future* (New York: Viking Press, 1968), 191.

7. There are a number of sociological studies done on the working class; among the ones I consulted are: *Blue-Collar Life* by Arthur Shostak, *Blue-Collar Aristocrats: Life-Styles at a Working Class Tavern* by E. E. LeMasters, and *The American School: A Sociological Analysis* by Patricia Cayo Sexton.

8. Urie Bronfenbrenner, "Socialization and Social Class Through Time and Space" in *Reading in Social Psychology,* 3d ed., edited by Eleanor Maccoby et al. (New York: Holt, 1958), 400–425.

CHAPTER 3

1. Helen Todd, "Why Children Work," *McClure's Magazine* 40 (April 1913): 68–79.

2. Selma Berrol, "Ethnicity and American Children," in *American Childhood,* edited by Joseph M. Hawes and N. Ray Hiner (Westport, Conn.: Greenwood Press, 1985), 350–51.

3. David B. Tyack, *The One Best System: A History of American Urban Education* (Cambridge, Mass.: Harvard University Press, 1974), 242.

4. Robert L. Reid, "The Professionalization of Public School Teachers: The Chicago Experience, 1895–1920," Ph.D. Dissertation, Northwestern University, 1968.

5. Selma Berrol, "The Schools of New York in Transition, 1889–1914," *The Urban Review* 1 (December 1966): 15.

6. David B. Tyack, "City Schools: Centralization of Control at the Turn of the Century," *Building the Organizational Society: Essays on Associational Activities in Modern America,* edited by Jerry Israel (New York: Free Press, 1972), 57–72.

7. Ibid., 65.

8. Selma Berrol has noted in her writings on the New York City schools how overworked teachers with 50 students in a class welcomed the absence of 20 students any day. However, high absentee rates did not reflect well on the school's record.

9. Modie J. Spiegel, "School Attendance from a Business Man's Viewpoint," in *The Child in the City,* edited by Sophonisba P. Breckinridge, 1912 reprint (New York: Arno Press, 1970), 167.

10. Marvin Lazerson and W. Norton Grubb, eds., *American Education and Vocationalism: A Documentary History* (New York: Columbia University Press, 1974).

11. David B. Tyack, ed., *Turning Points in American Educational History* (Waltham, Mass.: Blaisdell Publishing, 1967), 358–59.

12. Henry J. Perkinson, *The Imperfect Panacea: American Faith in Education, 1865–1965* (New York: Random House, 1968), 145.

13. Robert Bremner, "Rights of Children and Youth," in *Youth: Transition to Adulthood,* Report of the Panel on Youth of the President's Science Advisory Committee (Chicago: University of Chicago Press, 1974), 38.

14. Joseph Kett, "History of Age Grouping in America," Ibid., 27.

15. John Brooks, *The Great Leap: The Past Twenty-Five Years in America* (New York: Harper & Row, 1966), 229.

16. Eugenie C. Hausle, "Control of Extracurricular Activities in High School," *School and Society* 35 (April 2, 1932): 462. See also R. H. Eliassen, "The Teacher and Extra-Curricular Activities," *School Review* 40 (May 1932), 364–71.

17. Kett, "History of Age Grouping in America," 26.

18. Patricia Cayo Sexton, *Spanish Harlem* (New York: Harper & Row, 1965), 66.

19. Sara Solovitch, "Teenagers Are Passing up High School Life for Jobs," *The Philadelphia Inquirer* 315 (November 9, 1986): 1.

20. Ibid., 18-A.

CHAPTER 4

1. Hannah Arendt, "The Crisis in Education," 181.

2. Ibid., 181–82.

3. David Nasaw, *Children of the City: At Work and At Play* (Garden City, N.Y.: Anchor Press/Doubleday, 1985).

4. Ibid., 116.

5. Viviana A. Zelizer, *Pricing the Priceless Child: The Changing Social Value of Children* (New York: Basic Books, 1985).

6. Norman Ryder, "The Demography of Youth," *Report of the Panel on Youth* (Chicago: University of Chicago Press, 1974), 46.

7. Quoted in "A Time to Talk of Fads and Fruit Flies," *Business Week,* (August 28, 1971): 70.

8. "Fads of the Fifties," *Look* 24 (February 2, 1960): 83–88.

9. Gloria Steinem, "The Ins and Outs of Pop Culture," *Life* 59 (August 20, 1965): 72–73, 76.

10. "Rites, Styles, Passwords," *Newsweek* 67 (March 21, 1966): 75.

11. "A Time to Talk of Fads and Fruit Flies," 70.

12. Patrick Goldstein, "Will Hollywood Spoil Rock?" *Chicago Sun-Times,* May 7, 1978.

13. Patrick Goldstein, "FTC Doesn't Think Those Comic Book Ads Are Comical," *Chicago Sun-Times,* April 21, 1978.

14. Brian Sutton-Smith and B. G. Rosenberg, "Sixty Years of Historical Change in the Game Preferences of American Children," in *Child's Play,* edited by R. E. Herron and Brian Sutton-Smith (New York: John Wiley & Sons, 1971), 18–50.

15. Quoted in "The $25 Billion-a-Year Accent on Youth," *Newsweek* 64 (November 30, 1964): 80.

16. Grace Hechinger and Fred M. Hechinger, "In the Time It Takes You to Read These Lines the American Teenager Will Have Spent $2378.22," *Esquire* 64 (July 1965): 65–68, 113–14.

17. Ibid., 114.

18. Goldstein, "Will Hollywood Spoil Rock?" 1.

19. Cynthia Dagnal, "How Fame Kills Off Rock Stars," *Chicago Sun-Times,* November 20, 1977.

20. Norman J. Zierold, *The Child Stars* (New York: Coward-McCann, 1965), 64.

21. Ibid., 67.

22. George Frazier, "Frank Sinatra," *Life* 14 (May 13, 1943): 58.

23. Letters to the Editor, *Life* 41 (September 17, 1956): 19.

24. Bruce Bliven, "The Voice and the Kids," *The New Republic* 3 (November 6, 1944): 592.

25. E. J. Kahn, Jr., "Profiles: Phenomenon II, the Fave, the Fans, and the Friends," *New Yorker* 22 (November 2, 1946): 37–54; "A Farewell Squeal for Elvis," *Life* 45 (October 6, 1958): 77–80; *Business Week,* (August 22, 1964): 28–29.

26. Alex Inkeles, "American Perceptions," *Change* 9 (August 1977): 31–32.

27. Clifford Geertz, *The Interpretation of Cultures* (New York: Basic Books, 1973), 5.

CHAPTER 5

1. Edith Head, *How to Dress for Success* (New York: Random House, 1967), 3.

2. Joan Didion, "On Self Respect," in *Slouching Toward Bethlehem* (New York: Farrar, Straus and Giroux, 1968), 143.

3. Ibid., 145.

CHAPTER 6

1. Debby Miller, "Prince," *Rolling Stone* 394 (April 28, 1983): 18.

2. Ibid.

3. Ibid., 19.

4. Jim Miller, "The Peter Pan of Pop," *Newsweek* 101 (January 10, 1983): 52.

5. Vicki Davis, "Tracking U.S. Trends," *Chicago Sun-Times,* January 11, 1987.

6. Laurence Veysey, "Growing Up in America," in *American Issues,* edited by William T. Alderson (Nashville: American Association for State and Local History, 1976), 119.

7. Quoted in George F. Will, " 'New Collars,' New Values," *Newsweek* 108 (November 24, 1986): 100.

SELECT BIBLIOGRAPHY

Abbott, Edith, and Breckinridge, Sophonisba P. *The Delinquent Child and the Home.* Reprint. (New York: Arno Press, 1970).

Albin, Mel, and Cavallo, Dominick, eds. *Family Life in America, 1620–2000.* St. James, N.Y.: Revisionary Press, 1981.

Benedict, Ruth. "Continuities and Discontinuities in Cultural Conditioning." In *Personality and Nature, Society, and Culture,* edited by Clyde Kluckholm and Henry A. Murray. New York: Alfred A. Knopf, 1953.

Bernard, Jessie, ed. "Teen-Age Culture," *The Annals of the American Academy of Political and Social Science* 338 (November, 1961).

Bowles, Samuel, and Gintis, Herbert. *Schooling in Capitalist America: Educational Reform and the Contradictions of Economic Life.* New York: Basic Books, 1976.

Bremner, Robert H., ed. *Children and Youth in America: A Documentary History.* 3 vols. Cambridge, Mass.: Harvard University Press, 1970–1974.

Cochran, Thomas C. *American Business in the Twentieth Century.* Cambridge, Mass.: Harvard University Press, 1972.

_____. *Challenges to American Values: Society, Business, and Religion.* New York: Oxford University Press, 1985.

Cohen, Sol, ed. *Education in the United States: A Documentary History.* 5 vols. New York: Random House, 1974.

Degler, Carl. *At Odds: Women and the Family in America from the Revolution to the Present.* New York: Oxford University Press, 1980.

Erenberg, Lewis. *Steppin' Out: New York Nightlife and the Transformation of American Culture, 1890–1930.* Westport, Conn.: Greenwood Press, 1981.

Fass, Paula. *The Damned and the Beautiful: American Youth in the 1920s.* New York: Oxford University Press, 1977.

Finkelstein, Barbara, ed. *Regulated Children/Liberated Children: Education in Psychohistorical Perspective.* New York: Psychohistory Press, 1979.

Fox, Vivian C., and Quitt, Martin H., eds. *Loving, Parenting and Dying: The Family Cycle in England and America, Past and Present.* New York: Psychohistory Press, 1980.

Gedo, John E., and Goldberg, Arnold. *Models of the Mind: A Psychoanalytic Theory.* Chicago: University of Chicago Press, 1973.

Geertz, Clifford. *The Interpretation of Cultures.* New York: Basic Books, 1973.

Gilbert, James B. *Work without Salvation: America's Intellectuals and Industrial Alienation, 1880-1910.* Baltimore: Johns Hopkins University Press, 1977.

Gordon, Michael, ed. *The American Family in Social-Historical Perspective.* 2d ed. New York: St. Martin's Press, 1978.

Greeley, Andrew. "The Ethnic Miracle." *The Public Interest* 45 (Fall, 1976): 20–36.

Greven, Philip. *The Protestant Temperament: Patterns of Child-Rearing, Religious Experience, and the Self in Early America.* New York: Alfred A. Knopf, 1977.

Jones, George E. "America's Adults: In Search of What?" *U.S. News and World Report* (August 21, 1978): 56–9.

Kett, Joseph. *Rites of Passage: Adolescence in America: 1790 to the Present.* New York: Basic Books, 1977.

Lasch, Christopher. *Haven in a Heartless World: The Family Besieged.* New York: Basic Books, 1977.

Lazerson, Marvin, and Grubb, W. Norton. *American Education and Vocationalism: A Documentary History 1870-1970.* New York: Columbia University Press, 1974.

Levinson, Daniel J. "The Mid-Life Transition: A Period in Adult Psychosocial Development." *Psychiatry* 40 (May 1977): 99–112.

MacDonald, J. Frederick. " 'Hot Jazz,' The Jitterbug, and Misunderstanding: The Generation Gap in Swing 1935-1945." *Popular Music and Society* 2 (Fall, 1971): 43–54.

Murphey, Murray G. "An Approach to the Historical Study of National Character." In *Context and Meaning in Cultural Anthropology,* edited by Melford E. Spiro, 144–63. New York: Macmillan, 1965.

Peterson, Paul. *School Politics, Chicago Style.* Chicago: University of Chicago Press, 1976.

Rosenzweig, Roy. *Eight Hours for What We Will: Workers and Leisure in an Industrial City, 1870–1920.* Cambridge, England: Cambridge University Press, 1983.

Rothman, Ellen. "Sex and Self-Control: Middle Class Courtship in America, 1770–1870." *Journal of Social History* 15 (1982): 409–25.

Scott, Donald M., and Wishy, Bernard, eds. *America's Families: A Documentary History.* New York: Harper & Row, 1982.

Sennett, Richard. *The Fall of Public Man.* New York: Alfred A. Knopf, 1977.

Sexton, Patricia Cayo. *The American School: A Sociological Analysis.* Englewood Cliffs, N.J.: Prentice-Hall, 1967.

Stein, Howard F. "Identity and Transcendence." *School Review* 85 (May 1977): 349–75.

Tyack, David B. *The One Best System: A History of American Urban Education.* Cambridge, Mass.: Harvard University Press, 1974.

Vaillant, George F. *Adaptation to Life.* Boston: Little, Brown & Company, 1977.

Weiss, Nancy Pottishman. "Mother, The Invention of Necessity: Dr. Benjamin Spock's *Baby and Child Care,*" *American Quarterly* 29 (Winter, 1977): 519–46.

Welter, Barbara. *Dimity Convictions: The American Woman in the Nineteenth Century.* Athens: Ohio University Press, 1976.

Wiebe, Robert H. *The Segmented Society: An Introduction to the Meaning of America.* New York: Oxford University Press, 1975.

Winikoff, Beverly. "Changing Public Diet." *Human Nature,* January 1978, 60–65.

INDEX